FACTS AT YOUR FINGERTIPS

ANCIENT ROME

BROWN
BEAR
BOOKS

Published by Brown Bear Books Limited

An imprint of:
The Brown Reference Group Ltd
68 Topstone Road
Redding
Connecticut 06896
USA

www.brownreference.com

© 2009 The Brown Reference Group Ltd

Library of Congress Cataloging-in-Publication Data
available upon request

ISBN-13 978-1-933834-56-6

Editorial Director: Lindsey Lowe
Managing Editor: Tim Cooke
Design Manager: David Poole
Designer: Sarah Williams
Picture Manager: Sophie Mortimer
Picture Researcher: Sean Hannaway
Text Editor: Anita Dalal
Indexer: Indexing Specialists (UK) Ltd

Printed in the United States of America

Picture Credits

Abbreviations: AKG Archiv für Kunst und Geschichte,
London; BAL Bridgeman Art Library; C Corbis; MEPL Mary
Evans Picture Library; SPL Science Photo Library; b=bottom;
c=center; t=top; l=left; r=right.

Front Cover: Shutterstock: Irina Korshunova
Back Cover: iStockphoto: Lance Bellers

iStockphoto: Millsrymer 31, Amanda Lewis 34, Sophia
Tsibikaki 48, Serdar Yagci 54-55, Sergey Petrov 56, Noel
Powell 59; **Jupiter Images:** 19, 41, 44, 50; **Shutterstock:**
Ciara 1, 35, Kavram 5, Andrea Danti 8, Javarman 10, Asier
Villafranca 20, Eugene Mogilnikov 22, Holger Mette 29,
WitR 33, Adriaan Thomas Snaaijer 36, Allan Grosskrueger
38, Richard Southall 45, Falk Kienas 46, Afotoshop 51,
Connors Bros 54, Opis 58, Brent Wong 60; **Source:** 24.

Artwork © The Brown Reference Group Ltd

*The Brown Reference Group Ltd has made every effort to
trace copyright holders of the pictures used in this book.
Anyone having claims to ownership not identified above is
invited to contact The Brown Reference Group Ltd.*

CONTENTS

INTRODUCTION

This volume tells the story of the Roman Empire. It will help you step back 2,000 years and look at the Roman world. At its peak, the Roman Empire was home to 60 million people. The Romans were renowned for their military prowess, their buildings and feats of engineering, as well their contribution to language, arts, and culture. In many ways, the Roman Empire was perhaps the greatest ever created, and its influence is still felt today.

Roman achievements

The Romans invented many types of machinery and were able to survey and draw accurate plans, and then construct temples, aqueducts, roads and many other types of buildings and monuments, many of which survive today. The scale of their ambition and skill was breathtaking—for example, the Circus Maximus in Rome was a spectacular stadium that was erected for the staging of chariot races on a track that was 650 yards (600 m) long. The stadium could hold a staggering 350,000 spectators.

Writing and literature were introduced by the Romans into all the regions that became part of their Empire, from Britain in the north to Egypt and North Africa in the south. The Latin language was soon being used on a daily basis throughout the Roman world. People used it daily for business and for legal transactions. They were also able to enjoy plays at the theater and books—stories, histories, and poems. A great deal of Roman literature has survived until today because it was copied by monks in the Middle Ages from ancient original texts.

The Roman world

An important difference between the Roman Empire and most countries today is the large number of nations who lived there. Of the 60 million people who lived in the empire at its height, there were millions of people who had been brought into the Roman world by military conquest. These "new" Romans usually came to view themselves as Roman—certainly they were encouraged to do so, and to learn the standard Roman language, Latin.

Foundations of empire

In many ways, you could say that the Roman state was founded on slavery. Certainly there were large numbers of slaves owned throughout the Empire, on farms, in industries, and in homes. Many of them were badly treated, but most were well cared for.

The Roman world was large, and it covered a very long period in history. The Romans taught their children that Rome had been founded in 753 BCE; their Empire in the West was taken over by German armies in 476 CE. So Rome and the Roman way of life were important for more than 1,000 years.

This book outlines the history of the Roman Empire, shows how the Romans became the most important power in the world, and looks in detail at the effect they had on the lands they took over. Maps and photographs show the achievements of one of the greatest empires the world has ever seen.

Structure of the book

Ancient Rome is divided into two parts. The first describes the origins of Rome, its rise to dominate the Italian peninsula and the Mediterranean world, and the empire that stretched across Europe and into Asia and Africa. Part Two takes you on a tour of the different regions of the empire, with regional maps and guides to specific archaeological sites.

Abbreviations used in this book:
BCE = Before Common Era (also known as BC);
CE = Common Era (also known as AD);
c. = circa (about);
ft = foot;
cm = centimeter; m = meter; km = kilometer.
When referring to dates, early third century BCE., for example, means about 220 or 210 BCE, and late 3rd century BCE means about 290 or 280 BCE.

The aqueduct at Segovia in Spain is one of the outstanding surviving feats of Roman engineering. At its tallest, it is 93.5 feet (28.5 m) above the ground. The aqueduct was part of a system that used gravity to transport water to the city from a spring 10.6 miles (17 km) away.

TIMELINES

	600 BCE	500 BCE	400 BCE	300 BCE	200 BCE
ROME AND ITALY	Foundation of Rome 753 Tarquin I 616–579 Growth of the city *Villanovan hut urn, c.800 BCE*	Servius Tullius 579–534 Reorganization of the tribes, army, and constitution Tarquin II 534–509 Beginning of the republic 509 Rome most important town in Latium	Latins defeated at Lake Regillus 499 Invasions of Sabines, Aequi, and Volsci Domination of the patricians Campania overrun by Samnites 420 Siege and capture of Veii 405–396	Rome sacked by Gauls Latin War 340 Campania incorporated in Roman state 338 Roman colonization and conquest of Italy 334–264 Second Samnite War 327–304	Third Samnite War 298–290 Pyrrhus' invasion 280–275 Early Roman coinage (from c.280) First War with Carthage 264–241 Gauls invade Italy 225 Second War with Carthage 218–202 *The Capitoline Wolf, early 5th century BCE*	Direct taxation on Roman citizens abolished 167 Defeat of Cimbri and Teutones 102–101 *Coin of Hannibal, c.210 BCE*

Head of Apollo from Veii, c.500 BCE

	600 BCE	500 BCE	400 BCE	300 BCE	200 BCE
ART AND ARCHITECTURE	Primitive huts on the Palatine Rich tombs at Caere, Praeneste, etc. Roman Forum laid out; the first permanent stone buildings in Rome *Cylindrical "cist" (container), c.650 BCE*	Temples of Diana, Fortuna, and Mater Matuta c.560 Walls of Servius Tullius Temple of Jupiter Capitolinus 509 Etruscan tomb paintings	Temple of Saturn 497 Temple of Ceres 493 Temple of Castor 484 Temple of Apollo 431 *The "Lapis Niger," Rome's oldest public document, c.500 BCE*	Walls around Rome rebuilt 378 Via Appia, Aqua Appia built 312	Program of temple-building in Rome 302–272 Roman fine pottery industry flourishes Circus Flaminius 221	Greek art brought to Rome 200 Basilica Porcia built in the Roman Forum 184 Basilica Aemilia and Aemilian bridge 179 Temple of Fortuna at Praeneste c.120 *The circular temple in the Forum Boarium, late 2nd century BCE*

	600 BCE	500 BCE	400 BCE	300 BCE	200 BCE
LATIN LITERATURE		Earliest Latin inscriptions c.600	The Twelve Tables of Roman Laws written 451–450	Appius Claudius Caecus, politician Livius Andronicus, Naevius, Plautus, Ennius, Statius, Caecilius, and Pacuvius, playwrights and poets Cato, historian and scholar	Terence and Accius, playwrights L. Calpurnius Piso and Caelius Antipater, historians C. Gracchus, L. Crassus, and Q. Hortensius, lawyers and politicians

War with allies
91–89

Civil War: Sulla
dictator 83–82

Revolt of Spartacus
73–71

Civil War: Caesar
dictator 49–44

Murder of Caesar 44

Reign of Octavian/
Augustus
31 BCE–14 CE

Fire of Rome 64

Eruption of Vesuvius
79

*Augustus as
high priest, late
1st century BCE*

Antonine emperors
117–93

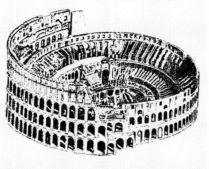

*The Colosseum,
79 CE*

Roman citizenship
extended to all
free inhabitants of
the provinces 212

"Great Persecution"
of Christians
303–05

Freedom of worship
restored 313

Constantine sole
ruler of the Empire
324–37

Division of the
Empire 395

*Diocletian and
Maximian,
c.300 CE*

Imperial court
shifted to Ravenna
402

Visigoths under
Alaric sack Rome
410

Rome pillaged by
Vandals 455

Last Roman emperor
of the west 476

Barbarian kings at
Ravenna 476–540

Byzantine
reconquest of
Italy 540

*Mosaic of Justinian at
Ravenna, c.560 CE*

Record office 78

Theater of Pompey
55

Forum of Caesar 46

Arch of Augustus 21

Baths of Agrippa 19

Theater of Marcellus
17

Forum of Augustus 2

*The triumphal arch
of Saintes*

Augustan building
program at Rome

Colosseum
dedicated 79

Trajan's Forum
dedicated 112

Pantheon rebuilt
118–28

Hadrian's Villa at
Tivoli 126–34

Severan building at
Leptis Magna

Baths of Caracalla
built at Rome 216

Aurelian builds walls
around Rome 271

*The "pastor
bonus" (Good
Shepherd)
sarcophagus,
early 4th
century CE*

Arch of Constantine

Church-building
programs at Rome,
Jerusalem, and
Constantinople

Mosaics in churches
at Ravenna

*Gold buckle from the
Thetford treasure,
Norfolk, England,
late 4th century CE*

Santa Sophia
rebuilt at
Constantinople
537

Cicero, lawyer and
philosopher

Caesar, lawyer and
historian

Lucretius, poet and
philosopher

Sallust and Livy,
historians

Catullus, Virgil,
Horace, Tibullus,
Propertius, and
Ovid, poets

Seneca the Elder,
orator

Persius, Lucan, and
Martial, poets

Pliny the Elder,
natural historian

Pliny the Younger,
letter writer

Tacitus, historian

Juvenal, poet

Suetonius, historian

Apuleius, novelist

Ulpian and
Papinian, lawyers

Tertullian, Christian
writer

Ausonius and
Claudian, poets

Ambrose, Jerome,
and Augustine,
Christian writers

Symmachus, orator

Ammianus
Marcellinus,
historian

Jerome translates
Old Testament into
Latin c.404

Orosius, historian

Servius and
Macrobius,
scholars

Theodosian code
compiled 429–37

Sidonius Apollinaris,
poet

Boethius,
philosopher

Cassiodorus,
historian and
administrator

THE ETRUSCANS

The Etruscans were a rich and powerful people who came from the area north of Rome, known as Etruria. They lived in the region centuries before the Romans. We know quite a lot about the Etruscans from the Romans and Greeks who were very interested in the earlier inhabitants. By the seventh century BCE, we know the Etruscans had created 12 separate states in the fertile hills of west-central Italy. Each state was independent with its own capital city, but they considered themselves to be Etruscan. When they came together, the states were very powerful. Gradually, they conquered other territories so that by the sixth century BCE, Etruscan territories extended as far north as Mantua and as far south as Salerno.

A rich and powerful people

Agriculture made the Etruscans rich. They increased their wealth through trade, mainly with the Greeks and others who wanted their technologically advanced metalwork and sophisticated pottery. The Etruscans built and lived in large cities with roads, sewage, and water systems. Many of the inventions credited to the Romans were actually invented by the Etruscans. For example, they created the system of aqueducts to transport water to cities.

Lost Language

We know less about the Etruscans than the Romans, because the Etruscan language was lost over time. In the second century CE, they were still speaking Etruscan and, although a few inscriptions survive to this day, they cannot be read. Most of our knowledge comes from the written records of the Romans and Greeks, which cannot be completely trusted.

The Etruscans were skilled builders who constructed stone arches and round, semi-underground homes, like this necropolis in Tuscany, with couches and chairs. The Romans based much of their own building on Etruscan engineering.

Etruscan tombs and art

However, in contrast to our lack of knowledge about the Etruscan language, much is known about Etruscan culture from the decorated underground tombs that they built for the rich citizens of their time. Their cemeteries were located outside the cities in special zones. Only the best architects, builders, and artists were employed to build these tombs.

The tombs were similar to underground houses. The walls and ceilings were decorated with colorful paintings, often showing the funeral ceremonies, which might have included open-air banquets with dancers, musicians, games, and sports. The tombs were even furnished. Above ground, the site of the tomb was marked with a high mound of earth.

The Etruscans believed in life after death, so their dead were buried with all of the things that they would need in the next life. Many of these grave objects, such as jewelry, statues, and vases, were magnificent.

BEGINNINGS OF ROME

The Etruscans were were just one of several peoples living in central Italy. The Samnites, Umbrians, Sabines, and Latins also lived there. The Latins were the largest group in Rome.

The Latin language

The Latins, who lived in the plain around and to the south of Rome, spoke Latin. We think that the Latin language came from across the Alps before the eighth century BCE. The language spread across the Roman Empire as it expanded. Latin forms the basis of many modern European languages, including English. Examples of words that originated from Latin include "civilian" (from the Latin *civis* or citizen of a town), "mile" (*mille passuum*, a thousand pieces), "family" (*familia*), and "second" (*secundus*).

Romulus, Remus, and early kings

The Romans believed their empire was founded by Romulus, the first ruler, whom they called *rex* or "king", who established the city on April 21, 753 BCE. According to legend, Romulus and his twin brother, Remus, were left in a basket on the Tiber River by a wicked relative. They were saved by a she-wolf who fed them. A royal shepherd then found them and he and his wife raised the boys as their own. According to legend, when the boys were older they founded Rome and the story continues with Romulus killing his brother during an argument.

The choice of the site for Rome was a good one. It was located by a river, surrounded by hills, and there was a lot of fresh water. We do not know whether Romulus and Remus really existed, but we do know that the first rulers of Rome came from both the Etruscan and Latin

This bronze statue, known as the "Capitoline Wolf", shows the she-wolf that kept Romulus and Remus alive by suckling them. The statue was made by an Etruscan artist in the sixth century BCE. The figures of the twins were added in the early 16th century CE., but it is likely that there were others there originally.

The Forum lay at the heart of Rome. Originally a marketplace that grew up between the city's hills, it grew into the business center of the city and was the site of many temples and monuments.

tribes. According to inscriptions, the names of the first three rulers were Numa Pompilius (a Sabine), Tullus Hostilius (a Latin), and Ancus Martius (a Sabine).

Three Etruscan kings followed. They were Lucius Tarquinius Priscus, Servius Tullius, and Lucius Tarquinius, who ruled for about 25 years. He was known as "Superbus," which meant "The Proud," because the people of Rome hated him. They got rid of him and created a new kind of government for themselves.

Government by elections

The Romans called their new government *respublica* ("republic"). It meant "a matter for the people". Every year, the citizens elected two officials, called consuls. The consuls had the same power as a king. They were head of the government and the army. They only held office for one year and they had to agree between themselves about how to govern.

Other officials also oversaw the process of governing. They included *praetors*, who were chief judges, *censors* who kept the register of citizens who could vote, *quaestors* who looked after the state's finances, and *aediles* who oversaw public works. The senate, a kind of parliament, was made up of former officials who discussed matters of state and advised the city's officials.

Citizens and conquest

The Romans were divided into social "classes". The noble families traced their ancestors back to early Rome. The plebeians were the ordinary working people. They were allowed to vote, but could not hold high office. Later, another class emerged. This was the *equites* ("knights"), who owned property and worked in business.

Not everyone was allowed to vote. Slaves and women could not vote, even though the system of government was democracy. In its earliest times, the Roman state was friendly with its neighbors, but eventually the Romans conquered them or forced them to become part of Rome. This began the process of expansion that created one of the world's greatest empires that, at its peak, included 60 million people.

Map showing Rome's allies and colonies. Allies often supplied troops to Rome. Colonies were set up by Roman citizens.

WAR WITH CARTHAGE

The Roman Republic continued to grow as the armies of Rome conquered all of Italy with the fall of Tarentum in 272 BCE. The Romans' strategy during the many Italian wars was to combine brutal warfare with generosity. If a rival state or community could not be incorporated into the Roman state (with either full or half-citizenship), it would be offered an alliance. Many Italian states willingly accepted this Roman offer in order to avoid full-scale military defeat. The Romans, for their part, were wise enough to not demand either taxes or tribute from the conquered states. Instead, the states were required to give their military assistance to Rome whenever required, which meant they lost their independence in foreign matters. However, the arrangement meant that were allowed to continue to run their own internal affairs.

When the Romans finally defeated King Pyrrhus of Epirus at Beneventum in 275 BCE, they became a major force in the Mediterranean region. However, they soon discovered that they were not the only "world power." In 264 BCE, the Romans, assisted by their Italian allies, went to war with the rival state of Carthage over an incident on the Mediterranean island of Sicily, which lay off the southern coast of Italy. Up to this point, the Carthaginians controlled North Africa and also part of Spain. They had then turned their attention toward Sicily and had started a campaign to conquer the island.

The first war

When the Carthaginians occupied present-day Messina (then known as Messana), the Romans sent soldiers to Sicily and the Carthaginians were defeated. However, the incident was just the start of a long-running war between Rome and Carthage that lasted for more than 20 years. A few years later, the Romans moved into the two other major Mediterranean islands of Corsica and Sardinia. The war between the two states ended in 241 BCE, following a battle off the west coast of Sicily. Rome emerged as the victor and then occupied Sicily, making the island its first province.

Hannibal—enemy of Rome

Hamilcar was the commander of Carthaginian forces at the end of the first war against Rome. In 237 BCE, his army defended Carthaginian territory in Spain, with the assistance of the local people who aided Hamilcar by supplying the farm produce and metals that fed and armed his troops.

Hamilcar had a son, Hannibal, and from an early age Hannibal was taught to hate the Romans. In 221 BCE, when he was only 25, Hannibal took over control of the Carthaginian armies in Spain. After two years of fighting, Hannibal conquered Rome's ally, the town of Saguntum. The Romans then sent two armies to confront the Carthaginians. One army was sent to Carthage (in present-day Tunisia) and the other to Massilia (now Marseille in France).

Battles between Rome and Carthage

First War

264 BCE Carthage occupies Messana. The Romans defeat the Carthaginians and occupy the town.

260 BCE Rome builds its fleet. Full-scale war.

241 BCE Carthage surrenders.

Second War

221 BCE Hannibal is made Carthaginian commander-in-chief

219 BCE Saguntum is captured. Rome declares war.

218 BCE Hannibal marches across the Alps. The Romans are defeated at Ticino and Trebia rivers.

217 BCE Two Roman legions are lost at Lake Trasimeno.

216 BCE Rome's worst defeat, at Cannae.

204 BCE Romans invade North Africa.

202 BCE Carthage defeated at Zama.

183 BCE Hannibal commits suicide.

Third War

149 BCE War breaks out again.

146 BCE The city of Carthage is completely destroyed. North Africa becomes a Roman province.

Crossing the Alps

In response, and to the amazement of the Romans, Hannibal then marched across the Alps to Italy with an army of 40,000 men and 37 war elephants. No one in Rome expected he would be able to cross the mountain range, and the march was very difficult, over treacherous terrain and in a harsh climate. By the time Hannibal arrived in Italy, only 26,000 men and 12 of the elephants had survived the journey. However, Hannibal was able to acquire more troops from some of the local tribes and then his revitalized army of 50,000 soldiers set about the task of trying to defeat the Romans on their own territory.

Campaign routes of the two "world powers." Both the Romans and the Carthaginians needed an efficient navy. At first, the Carthaginians had the naval advantage. Both sides also needed wealth to pay for the expensive wars and for their allies.

Rome saved

To deal with the impending threat from the invading Carthaginians, a new Roman general, Publius Cornelius Scipio, was appointed. In 203 BCE, after almost 15 years of fighting in Italy, Hannibal was recalled to Carthage to direct the defense of his homeland against a Roman invasion. Hannibal's army was defeated at Zama in 202 BCE. Hannibal is thought to have died in 183 BCE.

Within less than 100 years, the Romans had succeeded in destroying Carthage and had reduced the once mighty power to impotence. During the war, both sides had sustained huge losses. Estimates suggest that the Romans and its allies lost more than 100,000 men. They had also destroyed all the major powers of the Greek east and, by 167 BCE, the Romans were, in effect, the rulers of the Mediterranean region.

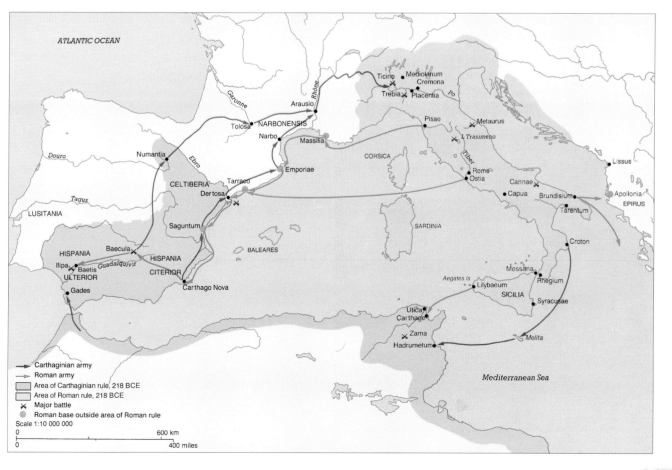

EARLY YEARS OF CRISIS

After a period of calm and stability, the Roman Empire came under serious threat of attack during the second century BCE along its northern and eastern borders. Three northern tribes—the Cimbri, Teutones, and Ambrones—threatened the security of Spain, southern Gaul, and Italy itself. In 105 BCE, an entire Roman army was killed at Arausio by these northern warriors and Italy lay at their mercy. This proved to be the lowest point for the Romans, as they faced up to the real prospect of Rome being completely destroyed.

Another severe threat to the power of Rome came with the revolt of the eastern provinces, when Mithridates VI (121-63 BCE), the king of Pontus, occupied Asia and the Greek islands. The local people in the Roman territory of Asia welcomed him in 88 BCE, because the Romans had treated them very badly. However, the Romans were determined not to lose their territory to Mithridates.

To resolve this crisis, the Romans had to depend on ambitious and determined men, who could rid them of their enemies. A brilliant and courageous consul, Cornelius Sulla (c.138-78 BCE), was given the task of

From 146 to 70 BCE, Rome faced difficulties throughout its empire. The period of crisis ended only when ambitious commanders such as Sulla and Pompey became powerful.

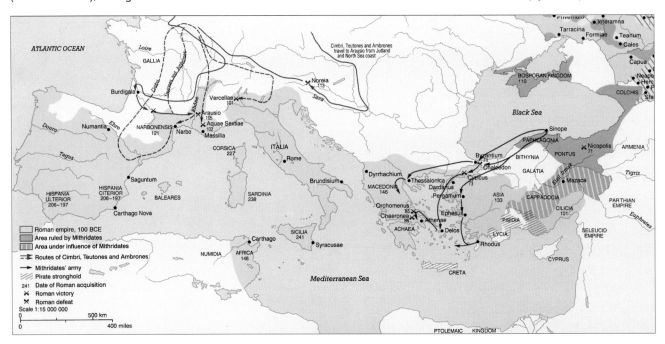

When the Romans refused to make their Italian allies Roman citizens, there was a revolt against Rome in 91 BCE. In 90 BCE., the Romans passed a law giving citizenship to loyal allies and others if they stopped fighting. The war ended in 89 BCE.

commanding a Roman army against Mithridates, despite some opposition to Sulla's appointment from within Rome itself.

When Sulla finally defeated Mithridates in 82 BCE, after a bitter four-year campaign, he returned to Rome and became a dictator who controlled the empire with an iron grip, taking revenge on those whom he perceived as being the enemies of Rome, including senior Roman nobles and officials.

Another serious threat to the Roman Empire came from the large bands of pirates who were based in the eastern Mediterranean and who plundered cities along the coasts of Greece and Asia. The pirates had even made attacks on Italy itself. They were not defeated until 67 BCE, when a resourceful Roman commander, Pompey, using a carefully orchestrated plan of campaign, finally conquered them.

Territory during the
Social War 91–89 BCE
- Roman
- Roman allies
- Latin
- Rebels

Scale 1:2 500 000

0 — 100 km
0 — 75 miles

REPUBLICAN ROME

The seven hills of Rome

As early as 1000 BCE, there were separate villages on the seven hills that surround Rome, the capital city of the Roman state. They united during Etruscan rule to become the first town of Rome about 575 BCE. The area of Rome that developed into the Forum dates from around 600 BCE. This was where Romans traded and conducted their business. As the town grew, the valleys that lead to the Tiber valley were covered with buildings. The port of Ostia was founded where the river led to the sea. Around 378 BCE, a wall was built to protect Rome. Experts think an early Roman emperor, Servius Tullius, built the wall. Unlike later Roman cities, Rome was not a planned city.

Rome expands

By the third century BCE, Rome had around 100,000 inhabitants. By Julius Caesar's rule, (c.100 BCE–44 BCE), the population had grown to almost one million. The poor lived in the lower levels of the valleys, often in squalor, while the rich moved to the hills where it was cooler and where disease was less prevalent. Cicero, the renowned Roman lawyer, orator, and and philosopher, wrote of the poor quality of living conditions at the time, noting that: "Two

Great stone aqueducts were built to bring water into Rome from the hills. The water was carried in a channel on the top. Rome's first aqueduct was built by the politician Appius Claudius in 312 BCE and named the Aqua Appia. The same man also built the Via Appia, a road from Rome to Capua.

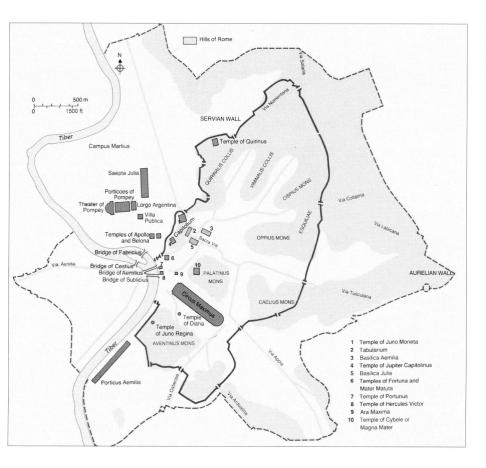

Map labels:

Hills of Rome
N
0 500 m
0 1500 ft
Tiber
SERVIAN WALL
Campus Martius
Temple of Quirinus
QUIRINALIS COLLIS
Saepta Julia
VIMINALIS COLLIS
Porticoes of Pompey
Theater of Pompey
Largo Argentina
Villa Publica
CISPIUS MONS
Via Salaria
Via Nomentana
Via Collatina
Via Labicana
Temples of Apollo and Belona
Capitolium
Sacra Via
OPPIUS MONS
ESQUILIAE
Bridge of Fabricius
Bridge of Cestius
Bridge of Aemilius
Bridge of Sublicius
PALATINUS MONS
AURELIAN WALL
Via Aurelia
Via Tusculana
Circus Maximus
CAELIUS MONS
Temple of Diana
Temple of Juno Regina
AVENTINUS MONS
Tiber
Via Ostiensis
Via Appia
Via Ardeatina
Porticus Aemilia

1 Temple of Juno Moneta
2 Tabularium
3 Basilica Aemilia
4 Temple of Jupiter Capitolinus
5 Basilica Julia
6 Temples of Fortuna and Mater Matuta
7 Temple of Portunus
8 Temple of Hercules Victor
9 Ara Maxima
10 Temple of Cybele or Magna Mater

of my apartment buildings have fallen down... even the mice have moved out!"

As the population of Rome grew, so did the demand for supplies of fresh water. Elaborate and ingeniously constructed stone aqueducts were built to convey the water from the nearby hills into the very heart of Rome. As the empire expanded, a series of stone roads were also built to link the city with its provinces.

Public buildings

By the end of the fourth century BCE, Rome had become rich and important. Magnificent buildings surrounded the Forum, and the town was dotted with other public squares. The city center also had a number of splendid temples. The opulence of the public buildings in the center of Rome contrasted sharply with the squalid tenement buildings most Romans lived in on the edges of the city.

Chariot racing was a popular spectator sport for the Roman population. By the first century BCE, 100,000 people watched the races in the impressive Circus Maximus. Vast warehouses and trading centers, such as the Porticus Aemilia, were built close to the river and marketplaces. Bridges, such as the Pons Fabricius which connected the left bank with Tiber island, were also built.

Rome's first stone theater was commissioned by Pompey and dedicated to him in 55 BCE. Sulla, Pompey, and Caesar each embarked on large construction projects, not only to radically change and improve the appearance of the city of Rome, but also to add to their own personal glory. Few of these monuments and temples from Republican Rome survive today. Successive Roman emperors knocked them down and replaced them with their own buildings, often reusing the stones.

RISE OF CAESAR

Julius Caesar believed he was descended from the gods. He claimed his ancestor was Aeneas, the hero of the Trojan Wars, whose mother was the goddess Venus. We think that Julius Caesar was born between 102 and 100 BCE into an important family of the Roman aristocracy. He had two sisters, but little else is known about his early life. Marius, a prominent politician and an enemy of the dictator Sulla was related to Caesar. The family connection proved valuable to Caesar's career, although it also brought him into conflict with the dictator.

A career in state service

Julius Caesar began his career in the army, which was typical for a Roman aristocrat. He served with distinction and when he returned to Rome, he began his political career. He held a number of public offices, such as head of Rome's financial affairs in Spain, and later he

Caesar wins the civil war of 49–45 BCE

49 BCE Caesar marches on Rome. In Spain, he destroys Pompey's army at Ilerda. Pompey flees to Greece.

48 BCE Pompey breaks through Caesar's defenses, but Caesar defeats him at the battle of Pharsalus. Pompey flees to Egypt, but is murdered before Caesar arrives.

47 BCE Caesar installs Cleopatra as queen in Egypt. Caesar then marches through Syria and Asia Minor to defeat Pharnaces of Pontus, an ally of Pompey, at Zela.

46 BCE After defeating Pompey's two sons at Thapsus, Caesar adds Africa Nova to the Roman Empire.

45 BCE Caesar defeats the Pompeian army at Munda.

Shown on the map is the territory added to the Roman state by Julius Caesar's conquests and the extent of his campaigns and wars. Caesar encouraged many Roman citizens and their families to set up colonies in the provinces.

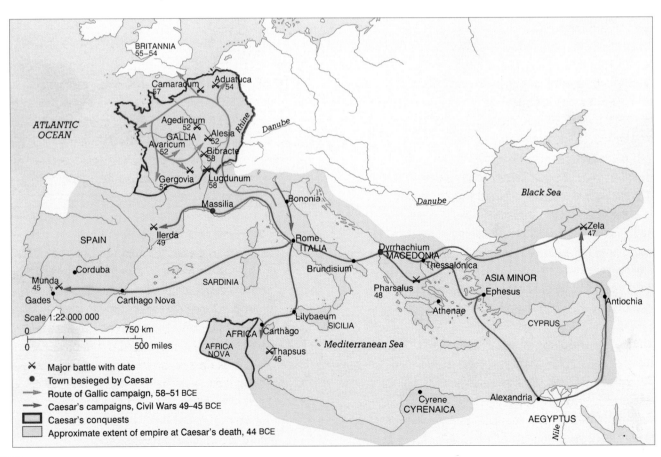

became responsible for all public building programs in Rome, as well as chief priest and a governor in Spain. He was elected to the highest office of consul in 60 BCE. His duties included control of the government and the army

Conquest of Gaul

When he had finished his year as consul, Caesar was in the position of being able to choose which province he wanted to govern. In 58 BCE, he became governor of northern Italy and Gaul, where he waged war against the Celtic people to make the region safer and also to expand Roman territory. By defeating the Celts, who were some of Rome's strongest opponents, Caesar opened up a route through Gaul. This prompted Cicero, the famous Roman speaker and philosopher, to address the Roman senate in praise of Caesar, saying, "Before, members of the senate, we only had a route through Gaul. All the other territories were occupied by peoples who either were hostile to us or could not be trusted. Caesar has fought very successfully against the fiercest of peoples in great battles and made them part of the Roman state."

Civil war and after

As a result of his military successes, Caesar found himself both popular and also deeply resented. When his rival Pompey persuaded the senate to order Caesar to break up his army in 49 BCE, a civil war erupted. It lasted for four

A sculpture of the Roman emperor Julius Caesar. The Roman writer Suetonius observed that Caesar was "a bit of a dandy. He always had his hair carefully trimmed and used to comb his few hairs forward to cover his baldness."

years. Caesar confronted Pompey in Greece where, in 48 BCE, he was triumphant, despite Pompey having a much larger army. Later, Caesar also defeated Pompey's sons in Spain. Returning home, Caesar became the most powerful person in Rome. He declared himself "dictator for life." This effectively meant that Rome was no longer a republic and that the people could no longer vote for their leaders, bringing an end to the concept of democracy.

Among Caesar's many acts as the ruler of Rome were numerous building programs, which included the construction of the Forum of Caesar, with its Temple of Venus Genetrix. One of his longest-lasting reforms was to the calendar. In 46 BCE, Caesar established the 365-day year, with a leap year every fourth year. The month of July is named after Julius in his honor.

The death of Caesar

However, as Caesar became grander in his ambitions, he began to make enemies in the Roman senate. When it emerged that Caesar was determined to award himself the title of *rex* (meaning king"), a group of his enemies, including such notable figures as Marcus Brutus and Gaius Cassius, began to plot against him, calling themselves "Liberators." In the end, they decided to kill Caesar. Summoning Caesar to the Senate on March 15, 44 BCE, they stabbed him to death on the steps outside.

EMPIRE OF AUGUSTUS

Although the Romans liked to think they still lived in a republic because they voted for their officials, in reality, power belonged to a few men. With the support of their armies, men such as Sulla, Pompey, and Julius Caesar took power and ruled like dictators. Following Caesar's murder, civil war erupted again in Rome. His adopted son and heir, Octavian, returned from Greece to avenge his father's murder.

The empire divided

Octavian and Marcus Antonius (better known as Mark Antony) emerged as the victors, and the Roman Empire was divided into two. Mark Antony ruled the east from Alexandria in Egypt, while Octavian ruled the remainder from Rome. However, Octavian and the Roman senate did not want the empire to stay divided, so they declared war against Antony and his lover, Queen Cleopatra of Egypt, in 31 BCE. Octavian declared victory for the Romans in 29 BCE.

Mighty Augustus

Octavian was now the most powerful man in the Roman Empire. In 27 BCE, the senate gave him

Augustus, the first emperor

March 15, 44 BCE Julius Caesar murdered. Civil war erupts.

31 BCE Octavian defeats Mark Antony and Queen Cleopatra at the battle of Actium in Achaen.

January 11, 29 BCE Octavian declares peace across the Roman Empire.

28 BCE Octavian is appointed *Princeps Senatus* (the leader of the senate). He now heads the state's armies and controls Rome's finances.

27 BCE Octavian is given title *Augustus*. The eighth month, *Sextilis*, is now renamed *Augustus* (August) in his honor.

23 BCE Augustus takes complete control of all provinces; then takes on more of the power of elected officials. Senate grants him extra powers.

15–13 BCE Augustus lives in Gaul.

2 BCE Augustus is given the title *Pater Patriae* (father of the country).

August 19, 14 CE Augustus dies at Nola.

September 17, 14 CE Senate decrees that the Emperor Augustus is one of the gods of Rome.

The Prima Porta statue of Emperor Augustus of Rome. Over 6 feet (2 m) in height and carved from marble, the statue was discovered in 1863 in the Villa of Livia at Prima Porta, near Rome. It depicts Augustus as the commander of the Roman army.

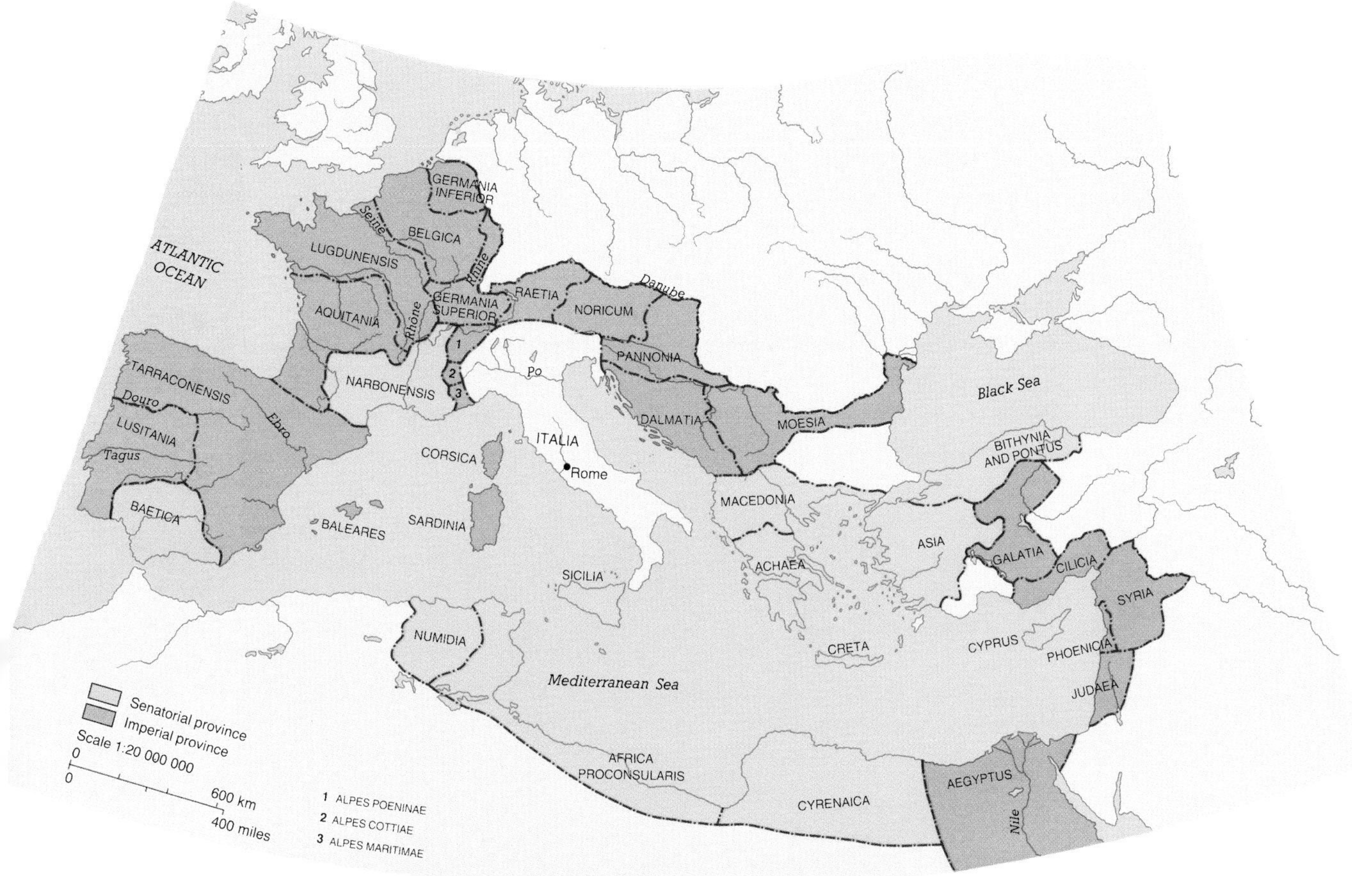
ATLANTIC OCEAN
GERMANIA INFERIOR
BELGICA
Seine
Rhine
LUGDUNENSIS
AQUITANIA
GERMANIA SUPERIOR
Rhône
RAETIA
NORICUM
Danube
PANNONIA
TARRACONENSIS
Douro
LUSITANIA
Tagus
Ebro
BAETICA
NARBONENSIS
Po
1
2
3
CORSICA
ITALIA
Rome
SARDINIA
BALEARES
DALMATIA
MOESIA
Black Sea
BITHYNIA AND PONTUS
MACEDONIA
ACHAEA
ASIA
GALATIA
CILICIA
SYRIA
SICILIA
NUMIDIA
CRETA
CYPRUS
PHOENICIA
JUDAEA
Mediterranean Sea
AFRICA PROCONSULARIS
CYRENAICA
AEGYPTUS
Nile
Senatorial province
Imperial province
Scale 1:20 000 000
600 km
400 miles
1 ALPES POENINAE
2 ALPES COTTIAE
3 ALPES MARITIMAE

The Roman Empire in 27 BCE. Out in the provinces, the local people's way of life became "Romanized." In 22 BCE, Augustus claimed that Narbonensis in Gaul was "more a part of Italy than a province." Legions of the Roman army were stationed throughout the empire (only a few remained in Italy), and this helped the spread of Roman customs.

the title "Augustus," which meant "a person to be respected," and the authority to control Rome's religious, civil, and military affairs. The senate acted as his advisors. Augustus then set about creating a powerful empire. He created a special force of soldiers who swore loyalty only to him. There may have been as many as 9,000 of these soldiers called the "Praetorian Guard." Augustus sent Roman legions to secure the borders in Spain and Germany. He divided the provinces into two types: the senatorial provinces, whose governors were appointed by the senate; and the imperial provinces, for which Augustus appointed the governors.

Governing the provinces

Augustus chose his imperial provinces very carefully. Most of the armies were based in these provinces and the governors he chose were loyal only to him. Augustus kept Egypt as his own personal property, even forbidding any Roman senator from traveling there without his express permission.

The governor's staff

A governor was called *Legatus* (appointed person) *Augusti* (by Augustus the Emperor) *pro Praetore* (in his place as governor). His title reflected his role, as he was the commander-in-chief, with as many as 40 officials reporting to him. They included military staff, secretaries, messengers, couriers, clerks, personal assistants, and lawyers, and as well as a procurator, who was responsible for the province's finances.

PROVINCES AND FRONTIERS

Following Augustus, several more emperors extended the Roman Empire further, expanding the vast territory controlled by Rome. In 43 CE, Emperor Claudius even participated personally in the invasion of Great Britain. He conquered Thracia and Mauretania as well. Emperor Trajan served as a soldier in many different parts of the empire and was a provincial governor before he became emperor. He also added new territories to the empire, including Dacia.

Guarding new frontiers

The Roman Empire reached its peak in the second century CE, when there may have been as many as 60 million people living within its frontiers. Around 450,000 soldiers, in 30 legions, were used to control this huge area. The

The Romans held together their empire by building thousands of miles of roads that made transportation far more efficient for goods—or for troops if trouble broke out in distant provinces.

soldiers were stationed at different frontiers, some as far away as Hadrian's Wall in northern England. The Emperor Hadrian built the wall to protect his empire from the Picts. Protecting the frontiers was very important and he traveled around the provinces of his empire, checking that they were secure from attack.

Roads and communications

The only way to maintain tight control over the vast areas of the Roman Empire was to ensure speedy and efficient communications. Troops had to be able to move quickly and at short notice to potential trouble spots, while couriers had to be able to transport messages as fast as possible to military command posts and to the emperor in Rome.

To facilitate communications of this nature, a vast network of roads was built across the empire. These roads were well constructed and could be used year-round in most weather conditions. Another important function of the road network was to transport goods efficiently around the empire. The roads soon acquired an economic importance, because taxes were levied on the commercial traffic that used them. Import taxes were payable at each provincial

New provinces gained by Rome

3rd century BCE: **241 BCE** Sicilia; **238 BCE** Sardinia; **227 BCE** Corsica.

2nd century BCE: **146 BCE** Greece and Africa; **133–129 BCE** Asia; **121 BCE** Gallia Narbonensis; **101 BCE** Cilicia.

1st century BCE: **74 BCE** Cyrenaica; **68–67 BCE** Creta; **64–63 BCE** Syria, Bithynia, and Pontus; **58 BCE** Cyprus; **58–52 BCE** Gallia; **30 BCE** Aegyptus; **27 BCE** Spanish provinces; **25 BCE** Galatia; **15 BCE** Alpes Poeninae; **14 BCE** Alpes Maritimae; **16-9 BCE** Raetia, Noricum, Pannonia, and Dalmatia.

1st and 2nd centuries CE: **6 CE** Judaea; **17 CE** Cappadocia; **40 CE** Mauretania; **43 CE** Britannia, Lycia, and Pamphylia; **46 CE** Thracia; **58 CE** Alpes Cottiae; **85–86 CE** Moesia divided into two provinces; **90 CE** Germania; **106 CE** Arabia and Dacia.

The provinces and frontiers of the Roman Empire to 106 CE. The empire covered a vast area of present-day Europe, the Mid-East, and North Africa, as well as the islands of the Mediterranean Sea.

frontier. However, it was often more economical to use the seas to move bulky goods across the empire. For example, it was cheaper to send corn by ships from Egypt and North Africa across the Mediterranean directly to Rome, rather than to transport it by much longer routes on the roads.

Imperial couriers

Augustus also created an official mail service, the *cursus publicus*, which not only carried mail, but also officials traveling on imperial business. To keep the roads in good condition and also to maintain the necessary horses and carriages on all the principal routes throughout the empire cost a lot of money. The cost of maintenance was partially the responsibility of the cities and towns through which the roads passed.

Traveling officials could make use of government rest-houses, known as *mansiones*. Other travelers had to make do with roadside inns. People who were rich enough might travel in a litter, called a *lectica*, which was carried by four strong bearers.

Journeys across the Roman Empire were slow, by modern-day standards. Strong walkers could cover about 20–25 miles (32–40 km) in a day, but those traveling on horseback or by coach would travel quicker. Imperial despatch riders, either on horseback or in chariots, would perhaps cover 40 miles (64 km) each day. The poet Horace wrote about one journey that he had made, saying, "We arrived quite worn out. It was to be expected. The journey was long, and the road conditions were awful because of heavy rain."

THE EMPERORS

The Romans believed in democracy. When they created their constitution, they did not include guidelines as to how an emperor should behave because the idea of a king (*rex*) went against the principle of democracy. They wanted to enjoy republican rule and elect their officials.

Last of the dictators

However, the Roman Empire experienced many moments of crisis when the Romans would turn to a strong leader to rule as a dictator. Often, a former consul was appointed, who took control of the government for a limited time. Julius Caesar was appointed dictator in 46 BCE.

When the civil war ended in 31 BCE, it was clear that the power of Caesar meant that the

The Roman Emperors

27 BCE –14 CE	Augustus
14–37	Tiberius
37–41	Gaius Caligula
41–54	Claudius
54–68	Nero
68–69	Galba
69	Otho, Vitellius
69–79	Vespasian
79–81	Titus
81–96	Domitian
96–98	Nerva
97–117	Trajan (97-98 with Nerva)
117–138	Hadrian
138–161	Antoninus Pius
161–180	Marcus Aurelius (161-169 with Lucius Verus)
180–192	Commodus
193	Pertinax
193	Didius Julianus
193–211	Septimius Severus
211–217	Caracalla (211-212 with Geta)
217–218	Macrinus
218–222	Elagabalus
222–235 CE	Alexander Severus

Disorder in the Roman Empire (235–284 CE)

235–238	Maximinus
238	Gordian I and II (in Africa)
238	Balbinus and Pupienus (in Italy)
238–244	Gordian III
244–249	Philip
249–251	Decius
251–253	Trebonianus Gallus
253	Aemilianus
253–260	Valerian
253–268	Gallienus (253-260 with Valerian)

WEST		EAST	
259–274	Gallic empire of Postumus, Victorinus, Tetricus	276–282	Probus
268–270	Claudius	282–283	Carus
270	Quintillus	283–284	Carinus and Numerian
270–275	Aurelian	260–272	Palmyrene empire of Odaenathus, Zenobia, Vaballath
275–276	Tacitus		

284–305 CE Diocletian and Tetrarchy

This mosaic picture is of the Emperor Justinian. He reconquered much of the western empire, which had been taken over by the Vandals in Africa, the Ostrogoths in Italy, and the Visigoths in Spain. The lands were gradually lost again.

The Roman Emperors (287–476 CE)

WEST	EAST
287–305 Maximian Augustus	284–305 Diocletian Augustus
293–305 Constantius Caesar	293–305 Galerius Caesar
305–306 Constantius Augustus	305–311 Galerius Augustus
305–306 Severus Caesar	305–309 Maximinus Caesar
(306-307 Augustus)	(309-313 Augustus)

306–312 Maxentius (Italy)

WEST	EAST
306–307 Constantine Caesar	308–324 Licinius Augustus
(from 307 Augustus)	

312–324 Constantine joint emperor with Licinius

324–337 Constantine sole ruler

337–340 Constantine II	Constans	337–361 Constantius II	
		351–354 Gallus Caesar	

355–361 Julian Caesar (360-363 Augustus)

361–363 Julian sole ruler

363–364 Jovian

364–75 Valentian	364–78 Valens
375–83 Gratian	379–95 Theodosius

375–392 Valentinian II (Italy, Illyricum)

WEST	EAST		
383–388 Maximus (usurper)			
392–394 Eugenius (usurper)	395–408 Arcadius		
395–423 Honorius (395-408 Stilicho as regent)			
421 Constantius III (with Honorius)	408–450 Theodosius II		
423–425 Iohannes (usurper)	450–457 Marcian		
425–455 Valentinian III	457–474 Leo		
455 Petronius Maximus	474–491 Zeno		
455–456 Avitus	475–476 Basiliscus)		
457–461 Majorian			
461–465 Libius Severus			
467–472 Anthemius			
472 Olybrius			
473 Glycerius			
473–475 Nepos			
475–476 Romulus Augustulus			

Barbarian rulers of Italy (CE)

476–493	Odoacer	491–518	Anastasius
493–526	Theoderic	518–527	Justin
526–534	Athalaric	527–565	Justinian
534–536	Theodahad		

empire could no longer be ruled by democracy. What Caesar and others did was to ensure their power base by gaining the support of the army.

First of the emperors

After he defeated Mark Antony during the civil war, Augustus became the first Roman emperor. Augustus (born Octavian) ushered in a period of 30 years of peace, and it was he who began the custom of giving formal titles to the emperor. The name "Augustus" meant "someone who is respected." It was given to him by the senate in 27 BCE. He also took the name of his adoptive father, Caesar. From then on, both "Augustus" and "Caesar" were titles that meant "emperor."

The Latin word for emperor—*imperator*—was originally bestowed upon successful military commanders, and it was later added to the titles Augustus and Caesar. Other formal titles were used to show respect to the emperor. Titles such as *Pater Patriae* ("Father of the Country") and *Princeps* ("First Citizen") appeared on coins and inscriptions, and in public announcements.

The good, the bad, and the mad

While some Roman emperors were good rulers, respected by their citizens, others were terrible. One of the greatest of the Roman emperors was Hadrian, who traveled widely across his empire and organized rebuilding on a large scale in every province. One of the worst emperors was Gaius Caligula. He was thought to be mad, as his alleged plan to make his favorite horse a Roman consul shows. Other emperors were cruel, murdering anyone who stood in their way and using public money for their own pleasures.

IMPERIAL ROME

When Augustus became emperor, the city of Rome had a population of more than one million people. Augustus realized that the city needed to be modernized. "I found Rome built of sun-dried bricks. I leave a city covered in marble," Augustus supposedly said at the end of his reign.

Augustus undertook a bold program to transform the city. He repaired the aqueducts and water systems, vital for the city's growing population's water supply. He built roads, a new senate house, and a theater for the local citizens to enjoy public performances. As well as repairing more than 80 temples, Augustus ordered new ones to built.

Two great fires

In 64 CE, during the reign of emperor Nero, a terrible fire destroyed much of Rome. The Roman historian Tacitus wrote that only 4 out of the 14 districts of Rome survived the devastation of the inferno.

Nero undertook a rebuilding program, which had at its heart an extravagant palace for him. According to the writer Suetonius, the palace, which stood in a huge park, was known as the Golden House, because parts of it were covered in real gold. When it was completed, Nero is supposed to have said, "Good, now I can live like a human being," which reflected his vanity. However, the palace did not stand for long. It was destroyed in another fire in 104 CE. Only a large statue of Nero in the entrance hall survived. The emperor Trajan later built his baths on the site of Nero's palace.

Aqueducts and baths

Other Roman emperors, as well as Augustus and Nero, were responsible for huge new building schemes. In 52 CE, Emperor Claudius finished an aqueduct that had been started by Caligula. The aqueduct, the Aqua Claudia, carried water over a distance of 40 miles (64 km) to Rome. The city needed a large volume of water, particularly for the bath complexes. Emperors Trajan, Caracalla, and Diocletian built the largest of the many bath complexes.

Forum and temples

The appearance of Roman cities changed after republican times. The biggest difference could be found around the city center, where the main forum was located. The forum, or main square, was where men carried out the business of the city. Located around the forum were basilicas, which were used as law courts, to hold meetings, or to carry out business.

In Imperial Rome, the forum became so important for the many ceremonies, both religious and secular, that were held there, that the forum was no longer permitted to be used for the buying and selling of goods, so new markets had to be built. The *forum boarium* ("cattle market") built near the Circus Maximus was one example of a new marketplace.

Many new temples were also erected in honor of the numerous different Roman gods. The temple of Venus and Roma was built near the site of Nero's palace in 135 CE, while the temple of Saturn was constructed on the edge of the forum. The temple of Juno Moneta was built on a hill overlooking the city. The word "Moneta" comes from the Latin term *monere*, meaning "to warn." The temple initially served as a watchtower, but it was later used as a place for minting coins. This is where the English word "money" comes from.

On the outskirts of Rome

While the center of the city of Rome was filled with many magnificent buildings and temples, the edges of the city were home to Rome's poor, many of whom lived in squalid slum dwellings. As the city grew, a new wall was then needed to protect it, and in the third century CE such a wall was constructed. The Aurelian Wall was the first to encircle the Roman army camp where the troops who protected the emperor were based.

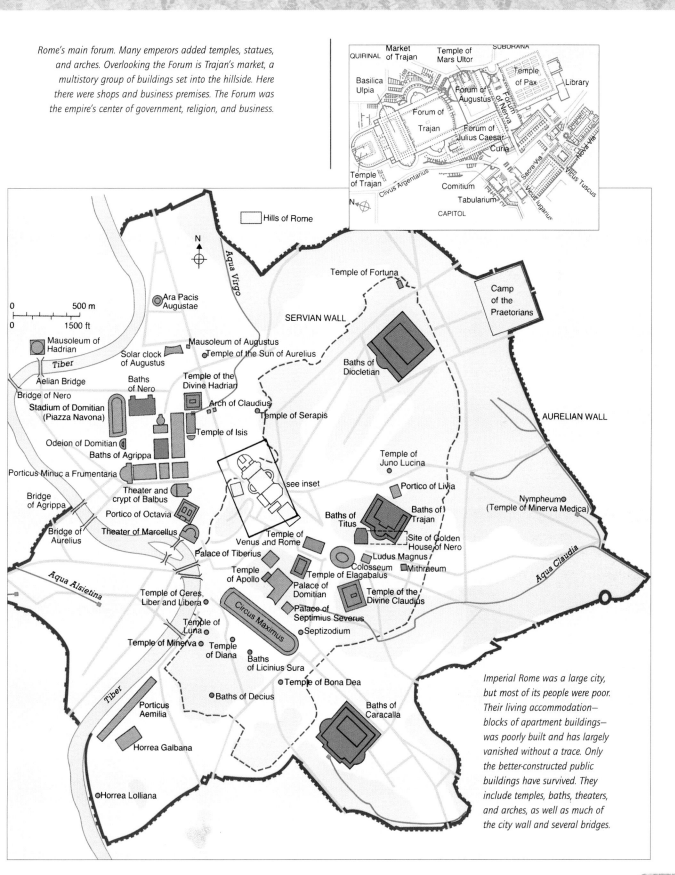

Rome's main forum. Many emperors added temples, statues, and arches. Overlooking the Forum is Trajan's market, a multistory group of buildings set into the hillside. Here there were shops and business premises. The Forum was the empire's center of government, religion, and business.

QUIRINAL Market of Trajan — Temple of Mars Ultor — SUBURANA
Basilica Ulpia — Temple of Pax — Library
Forum of Augustus
Forum of Nerva
Forum of Trajan
Forum of Julius Caesar
Temple of Trajan — Curia
Clivus Argentarius
Comitium
Sacra Via
Vicus Tuscus
Nova Via
Tabularium
Vicus Jugarius
N
CAPITOL

Hills of Rome

N

0 500 m
0 1500 ft

Aqua Virgo

Temple of Fortuna

SERVIAN WALL

Camp of the Praetorians

Ara Pacis Augustae

Mausoleum of Hadrian
Tiber
Aelian Bridge
Bridge of Nero
Stadium of Domitian (Piazza Navona)
Odeion of Domitian
Baths of Agrippa
Porticus Minuc a Frumentaria
Bridge of Agrippa
Portico of Octavia
Theater of Marcellus
Bridge of Aurelius

Mausoleum of Augustus
Solar clock of Augustus
Temple of the Sun of Aurelius
Baths of Nero
Temple of the Divine Hadrian
Arch of Claudius
Temple of Serapis
Temple of Isis

Baths of Diocletian

AURELIAN WALL

Temple of Juno Lucina

Portico of Livia

Nympheum (Temple of Minerva Medica)

see inset

Theater and crypt of Balbus

Baths of Titus
Baths of Trajan

Site of Golden House of Nero

Temple of Venus and Rome
Palace of Tiberius
Temple of Apollo
Temple of Ceres, Liber and Libera
Temple of Luna
Temple of Minerva
Temple of Diana

Ludus Magnus
Colosseum
Mithraeum
Temple of Elagabalus
Palace of Domitian
Palace of Septimius Severus
Septizodium

Temple of the Divine Claudius

Aqua Claudia

Circus Maximus

Aqua Alsietina

Baths of Licinius Sura
Temple of Bona Dea
Baths of Decius
Baths of Caracalla

Tiber
Porticus Aemilia
Horrea Galbana

Horrea Lolliana

Imperial Rome was a large city, but most of its people were poor. Their living accommodation—blocks of apartment buildings—was poorly built and has largely vanished without a trace. Only the better-constructed public buildings have survived. They include temples, baths, theaters, and arches, as well as much of the city wall and several bridges.

THE LATER EMPIRE

During the third century CE, the Roman Empire began to fall into disunity as frequent uprisings seriously threatened the stability of Roman rule. The Romans were obliged to construct new forts along the coasts of Britain and Gaul in order to protect their territory. The political instability of the time is perhaps best illustrated by the fact that between 235 CE and 284 CE there were more than 18 emperors. None of them ruled for more than a few years before they were either murdered or expelled.

The legions elect Diocletian

A significant moment in the entire history of the Roman Empire was the election of Diocletian as emperor in 284 CE. Diocletian came from the province of Dalmatia and was the commander of Emperor Numerian's bodyguard. Following Numerian's murder, the Roman army chose Diocletian to become the next emperor.

The Reforms of Diocletian

211 CE Emperor Septimius Severus dies in York. There are now 46 provinces in the Roman Empire, but many are later subdivided.

284 CE Diocletian is declared emperor.

286 CE Maximian is made emperor in the west.

293 CE Diocletian creates the "rule of four men" – two emperors and two successors.

296 CE Diocletian reorganizes the empire's finances. Fixed prices are introduced for coins of gold, silver, and bronze. All coin minting is now done by the state. New tax system is introduced.

301 CE Diocletian introduces an official price list for goods. The system is later abandoned as unworkable.

303 CE Diocletian gives up his throne because of ill health.

313 CE Diocletian dies.

314 CE The Roman Empire now has 101 provinces.

330 CE Emperor Constantine the Great moves the capital of a reunited Roman Empire to Constantinople.

Reorganization of the empire

Diocletian proved to be a decisive ruler who oversaw the transformation of the Roman Empire. He divided it into two and ruled the eastern empire from Nicomedia in Bithnyia. He chose his friend Maximian to rule from Rome in the west. In 293 CE, Diocletian introduced further reforms when he set up a tetrarchy, or "four-man" rule. He appointed two successors, Galerius and Constantius, one for Maximian and one for him, to help run the empire. The two emperors adopted their respective successors.

The plan worked well and the empire ran sufficiently well that Diocletian did not have to visit Rome for a period of 10 years. He spent some of his time in Egypt, where he suppressed a revolt. Meanwhile Maximian suppressed a similar uprising in Mauretania and Constantius unseated a usurper in Britain. Galerius fought against the Goths on the lower Danube and spectacularly defeated the Persians in 297–298. He established the frontier of the empire along the upper Tigris as far east as Kurdistan and Singara.

The system worked so well that Diocletian's government and political reforms remained stable for over 20 years. In 305 Diocletian and Maximian resigned and Galerius and Constantius became emperors. They in turn each appointed a successor, in an attempt to continue the success of the Tetrarchy. However, this time the arrangement collapsed.

Reorganization of the army

Diocletian reorganized the empire into 12 districts, each with its own governor, called a *vicarius*. Diocletian also increased the size of the Roman army. Some contemporary witnesses say that he quadrupled it, although most modern historians estimate that he may have doubled it. He stationed troops permanently along the empire's frontiers and introduced smaller units of mobile troops that could be moved at short notice to wherever they were

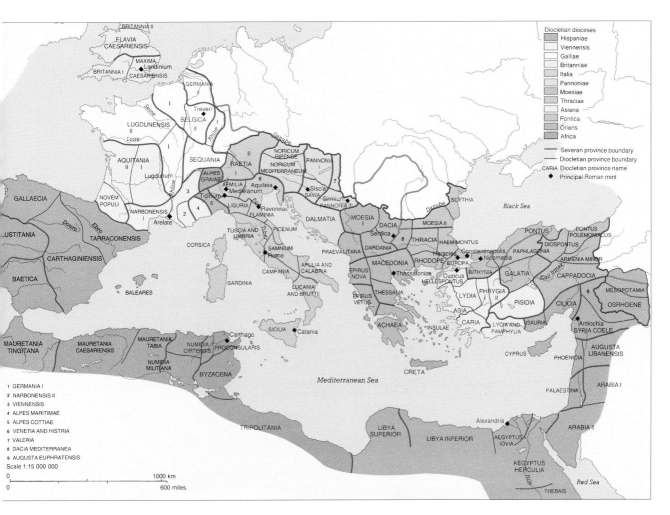

The Roman Empire as ruled by Diocletian. His system of "four-man" rule brought stability to Roman lands.

needed. Some of the frontier troops were essentially local militia, who received land in return for performing military duty.

The increase in the size of the army had to be paid for through taxation. Diocletian attempted to stabilize the economy. Among his other reforms was to overcome inflation by setting up an official price list for goods sold throughout the empire. Anyone who did not stick to the price list could in theory be punished by death or exile. In practice, the reform ultimately proved unworkable.

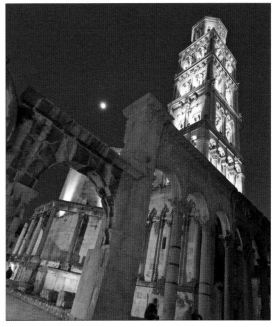

Diocletian built himself a palace in Split, in modern Croatia, in preparation for his retirement as emperor in 305.

GEOGRAPHY OF THE EMPIRE

At its peak in 117 CE, the Roman empire covered most of Europe and the whole coast of the Mediterranean Sea. The Romans brought some standardisation throughout the empire. They built colosseums, public baths and paved roads, for example, and introduced the Latin language. Still, different regions of the empire had different characters: northern Britain was greatly different from the edges of the Sahara Desert, for example.

This section of the book introduces the major regions of the empire in a series of map spreads. Supplementary spreads give details of major specific Roman sites from the region.

The Via Appia was built in the fourth century BCE to connect Rome to Brindisi, a major port for trade with Greece and the eastern Mediterranean.

AFRICA

Following the Roman destruction of Carthage, which lies in present-day Tunisia in North Africa, the Romans began to rule the province of Africa in 146 CE. Initially, the province was made up of just Tunisia, but, before long, Roman rule was extended, so that Roman territory reached from Libya in the east to Morocco in the west. Mountains and deserts formed a natural barrier to the south and marked the southern edge of the Roman province.

Exporting to the empire

The province of Africa was the breadbasket of the Roman Empire. The region was very rich, due to its fertile land. At one time, the province supplied two-thirds of Rome's corn needs. It was also a major supplier of olives and olive oil, products that were very important to the Roman Empire. Archeologists have excavated olive presses and large storage jars sunk into the ground in many of the villas built during Roman rule in North Africa.

Another major export to Rome was wild animals. The amphitheatres across the empire relied on a supply of exotic wild animals for the entertainment of the Roman public. Animals that were exported from North Africa included leopards, wild asses, rhinos, lions, elephants, antelopes, zebra, giraffes, and ostriches.

Around 28,000 Romans soldiers were stationed in North Africa and it was the Roman army that enabled the province to become such a prosperous part of the empire. The soldiers kept the peace in the region by building a series of forts and camps from which they carried out regular patrols of the territory. The land was

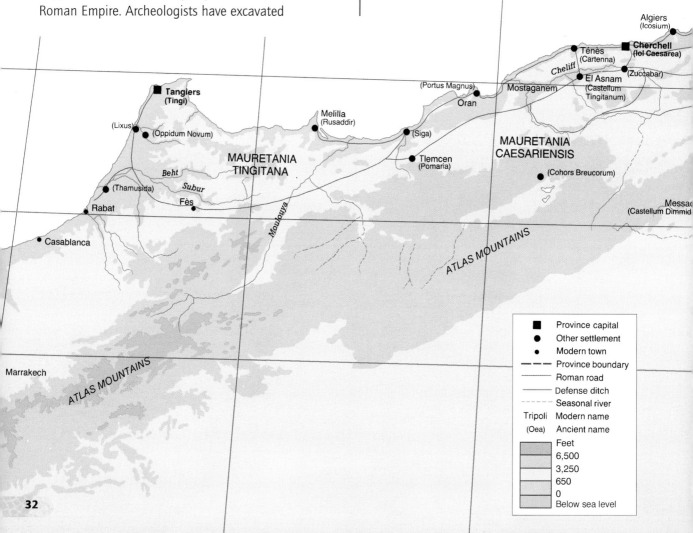

Algiers
(Icosium)

Ténès
(Cartenna)

Cherchell
(Iol Caesarea)

Cheliff

(Zuccabar)

El Asnam
(Castellum
Tingitanum)

(Portus Magnus)

Mostaganem

Oran

Tangiers
(Tingi)

Melilla
(Rusaddir)

(Lixus)

(Oppidum Novum)

(Siga)

MAURETANIA
CAESARIENSIS

MAURETANIA
TINGITANA

Tlemcen
(Pomaria)

Beht

Subur

(Thamusida)

(Cohors Breucorum)

Fès

Rabat

Moulouya

Messa
(Castellum Dimmid

Casablanca

ATLAS MOUNTAINS

Marrakech

ATLAS MOUNTAINS

■	Province capital
●	Other settlement
•	Modern town
– – –	Province boundary
——	Roman road
——	Defense ditch
-----	Seasonal river
Tripoli	Modern name
(Oea)	Ancient name

Feet
6,500
3,250
650
0
Below sea level

divided up into plots and huge farming estates were created. Often, these belonged to the emperor or to rich people who lived in Rome.

New colonies

Before the Romans arrived there were a number of towns scattered along the North African coast. Hannibal had ruled the region from the city of Carthage. Once the Romans arrived, in the west, in Mauretania, Emperor Augustus created 12 new colonies for retired Roman soldiers and their families. These families lived according to the Roman way of life, but the indigenous people of the region continued to speak their own language and follow some of their own customs.

An arched doorway marks the entrance to a market in the Roman colony of Leptis Magna in what is now Libya. The city grew wealthy through trade with Rome and the Italian peninsula.

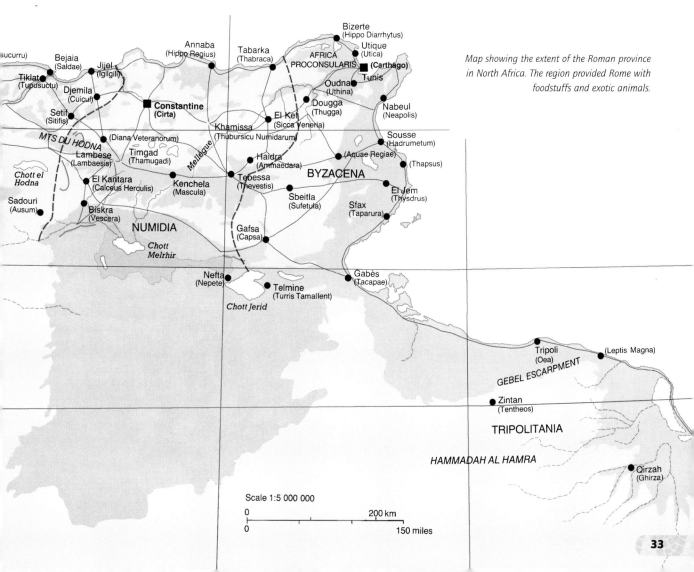

Map showing the extent of the Roman province in North Africa. The region provided Rome with foodstuffs and exotic animals.

Leptis Magna

Leptis Magna lies on the coast of North Africa. It may have been founded as early as the fifth century BCE by

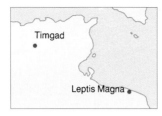

the Phoenicians. They built it close to the well-protected harbor, which had a lighthouse and a beacon to guide ships. Although Rome was far away, Leptis exported to the capital goods such as corn and olive oil.

Fine buildings

The wealth of Leptis Magna, earned from trade and agriculture, was clear in its magnificent buildings. Emperor Septimius Severus was born in the town and he was responsible for building a new harbor there, as well as a colonnaded forum and a basilica. Emperor Hadrian later built an impressive street with colonnades on either side from the harbor to the public baths. Leptis Magna was the third most important city in Africa after Carthage and Alexandria.

When Emperor Septimius returned to the city of his birth in 203 CE, the people marked the visit by erecting a huge memorial arch at a crossroads that was visible from miles away.

Leptis Magna is remarkably well preserved. Many colonnades and remnants of its buildings, such as the theater, survived because they were covered by sand dunes over time.

In 1 CE, this theater was built by a rich nobleman in Leptis Magna in North Africa. The columns on the right are part of a temple. The photograph clearly shows the close proximity of Leptis Magna to the Mediterranean Sea, which can be seen in the background.

Timgad

Timgad, situated in present-day Algeria, was a new town founded by the Romans originally as a colony for retired soldiers of the Third Legion in 100 CE, which was stationed at Lambaesis nearby. The town lies on the edge of a desert, and, like many Roman towns, it was laid out like an army fort. Almost exactly square-shaped, each side of the town measured approximately 385 yards (350 m) long.

In typical Roman style, Timgad was divided up into regular blocks (known as *insulae*). The town was made up of 111 blocks all of which were about the same size. This grid system allowed for easy access and transportation throughout the town. Roman forts were planned in a similar way.

Housing for the army veterans and their families made up most of the accommodation. To begin with, there was little room for public buildings within the downtown area. The original plans did, however, include both a forum and a theater, which were constructed close to the crossroads where the two main streets met in the center of Timgad. The town also had a marketplace and a building for public baths.

Growth and success

As Timgad grew wealthier and attracted more residents, the growing population wanted the same amenities enjoyed by Roman citizens elsewhere. Town planners accepted that they would need to build outside the confines of the original site. Additional public buildings were added from the mid-second century CE onward. The new structures included a total of 13 public baths, a library, temples, a clothes market, and a triumphal arch. As the population expanded, so more housing became necessary and the town council allowed for new residential buildings to be constructed outside the town limits. The original city wall was taken down and the town was expanded to the west and north. The new buildings, however, did not

This Gorgon's head was carved on the new forum built in Leptis Magna by the emperor Septimius Severus. The emperor had been born in the city, and was later commemorated there by a massive ceremonial arch.

follow the strict grid pattern of the original town layout.

Timgad was a wealthy town because of the fertile farming land around it and, as the town grew and prospered, it helped to transform the frontier into a peaceful area.

SPAIN AND PORTUGAL

When the Romans first conquered Spain, they settled in the south, around the River Baetis (now known as Guadalquivir River) and along eastern seaboard. The mountains to the north and northwest remained free of Roman control until the Cantabrian wars of Emperor Augustus. In order to pacify the people of these regions, they were allowed to keep much of their culture and language. The Basque language, which is still spoken today, is a pre-Roman language.

Following Emperor Augustus's conquest of the Iberian Peninsula (made up of the present-day countries of Spain and Portugal), he divided the region up into three provinces. Even though the people quickly adopted Roman ways, one army legion was kept in the Basque region in the north of the Iberian Peninsula to put down any possible rebellions.

The oldest and most famous town in Roman Spain was Italica, where both the future Roman emperors Trajan and Hadrian were born. It was originally founded in 206 BCE as a place for soldiers who were injured in the battle of Illipa. The town was later redesigned during Hadrian's rule into an impressive city with colonnaded streets and a large amphitheater.

Mines, wines, and fish sauce

In the first century CE, the Roman writer Pliny said, "Almost all of Spain has mines producing lead, iron, tin, silver, and gold." There were also copper mines. As well as mines, the Spanish

This stone aqueduct brought water to the city of Segovia from Riofrio, 10 miles (16km) away. Its arches stretched nearly 1 mile (1.6km) to carry water (at the very top, 100ft/30m above the ground) across the city.

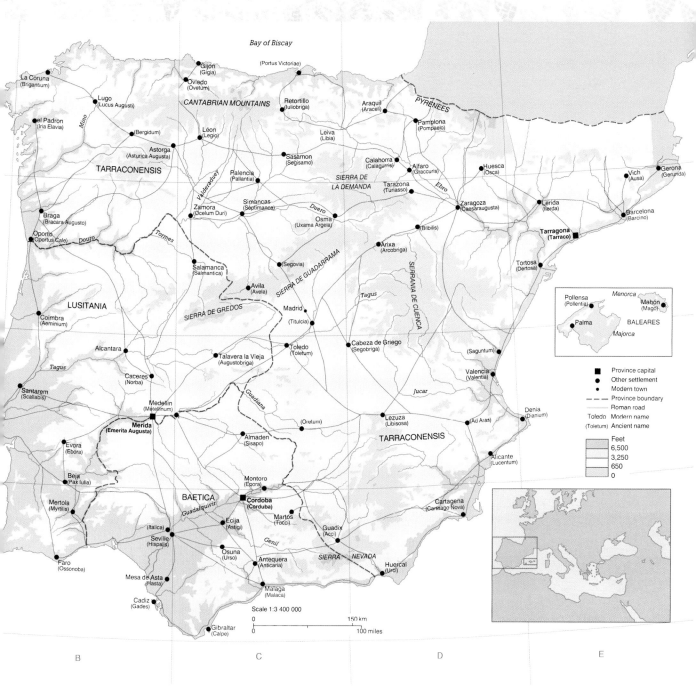

Bay of Biscay

La Coruña
(Brigantium)

Gijón
(Gigia)

(Portus Victoriae)

Oviedo
(Ovetum)

Lugo
(Lucus Augusti)

CANTABRIAN MOUNTAINS

Retortillo
(Iuliobriga)

Araquil
(Araceli)

PYRENEES

el Padron
(Iria Elavia)

Miño

León
(Legio)

(Bergidum)

Léon
(Legio)

Leiva
(Libia)

Pamplona
(Pompaelo)

Astorga
(Asturica Augusta)

Sasamón
(Segisamo)

Calahorra
(Calagurris)

Alfaro
(Graccuris)

Huesca
(Osca)

Vich
(Ausa)

Gerona
(Gerunda)

TARRACONENSIS

Valdeaduey

Palencia
(Pallantia)

SIERRA DE
LA DEMANDA

Tarazona
(Turiasso)

Ebro

Zaragoza
(Caesaraugusta)

Lérida
(Ilerda)

Barcelona
(Barcino)

Braga
(Bracara Augusto)

Zamora
(Ocelum Duri)

Simancas
(Septimanca)

Duero

Osma
(Uxama Argela)

(Bilbilis)

TARRAGONA
(Tarraco)

Tortosa
(Dertosa)

Oporto
(Oportus Cale)

Douro

Tormes

Arixa
(Arcobriga)

Salamanca
(Salmantica)

(Segovia)

SIERRA DE GUADARRAMA

SERRANIA DE CUENCA

Avila
(Avela)

LUSITANIA

SIERRA DE GREDOS

Madrid

(Titulcia)

Tagus

Coimbra
(Aeminium)

Alcantara

Toledo
(Toletum)

Talavera la Vieja
(Augustobriga)

Cabeza de Griego
(Segobriga)

(Saguntum)

Tagus

Caceres
(Norba)

Valencia
(Valentia)

Santarem
(Scallabis)

Medellin
(Metellinum)

Guadiana

Jucar

Denia
(Dianium)

Mérida
(Emerita Augusta)

Evora
(Ebora)

Almaden
(Sisapo)

(Oretum)

Lezuza
(Libisosa)

(Ad Aras)

TARRACONENSIS

Alicante
(Lucentum)

Beja
(Pax Iulia)

Montoro
(Epora)

BAETICA

Cordoba
(Corduba)

Cartagena
(Carthago Nova)

Mertola
(Myrtilis)

Guadalquivir

(Italica)

Ecija
(Astigi)

Martos
(Tucci)

Guadix
(Acci)

Faro
(Ossonoba)

Seville
(Hispalis)

Genil

Osuna
(Urso)

Antequera
(Anticaria)

SIERRA NEVADA

Huercal
(Urci)

Mesa de Asta
(Hasta)

Malaga
(Malaca)

Cadiz
(Gades)

Gibraltar
(Calpe)

Scale 1:3 400 000

0   150 km
0   100 miles

Pollensa
(Pollentia)

Menorca

Mahón
(Mago)

Palma

BALEARES

Majorca

■ Province capital
● Other settlement
• Modern town
--- Province boundary
—— Roman road
Toledo Modern name
(Toletum) Ancient name

Feet
6,500
3,250
650
0

B   C   D   E

provinces exported vast quantities of olive oil and wine, both vitally important agricultural products to the Roman Empire. The Spanish province was famous throughout the Roman Empire for one product called *garum*. This was a highly-prized salted fish sauce that was used in many Roman recipes.

The Romans required all its provinces to produce wealth for the state, and during the empire, the state owned most of the Spanish

In the far west of the Roman Empire, Spain was an important source of wealth for the Romans.

mines. However, despite its economic and social importance, Spain played little role in the political events of the Roman Empire. This was largely a result of the small numbers of soldiers stationed in the province. It was not until the early fifth century CE that rebellion in Spain heralded the collapse of the Roman Empire.

GAUL AND GERMANY

A Roman historian, Ammianus Marcellinus, who lived in the fourth century CE, wrote, "Nearly all the Gauls are tall, fair-haired, and have a ruddy complexion. They are always quarrelling and are proud and insolent." The Gauls lived in Gallia (present-day France) close to Germania (modern-day Germany), and both of these regions were home to a number of Celtic-speaking peoples.

Some of these regions had been conquered before the Romans arrived. In the far south of Gallia, the Greeks established Massilia (the present-day city of Marseille) as early as 600 BCE. As a result, there was a marked contrast between the urbanized south of Gallia and the regions north and west of the Massif Central mountain range, known as Gallia Comata.

Later, Julius Caesar conquered a huge area to the north and extended the Roman Empire as far as the Atlantic Ocean, to the west. Caesar used northern Gallia as the launchpad for his first invasion of Britain in 55 BCE.

"Long-haired Gaul"

The regions of Gallia and Germania were sub-divided by the Romans into three distinct parts. In the south, the existing settlements were enlarged and transformed into Roman towns. Spectacular Roman remains survive today in the South of France in towns such as Nîmes, Arles, and Orange. The biggest town in the region was Lyon, while an important port was built at Narbonne on the Mediterranean coast.

In Germania, close to the River Rhine, the Romans created several new colonies for retired soldiers, as well as a number of forts to protect their new frontier. The Romans called the north and west area "Gallia Comata" (which translates as "long-haired Gaul"). The land was very fertile and the wide open spaces were perfect for agriculture. There were large farming estates that were worked on by the local population. Impressive villas, such as the Estrées-sur-Noye, dotted the landscape.

The Porta Nigra, or "Black Gate," at Trier in Germany was built in the second century CE as the entrance to the city for travelers approaching from the north. The gate got its name in the Middle Ages from the dark color of its stonework.

During the later Roman Empire, there was a shift in the balance of trading power from the south to the north. This change was mainly because of the presence of an imperial court at Trier (Augusta Treverorum), which attracted increased financial and material resources.

The Alps mountains comprise a barrier dividing France from Italy. The Romans would talk about "this side" (their side) or "the other side" of the Alps. In France, the earliest Roman towns were in "the Province" — today the region is known as Provence.

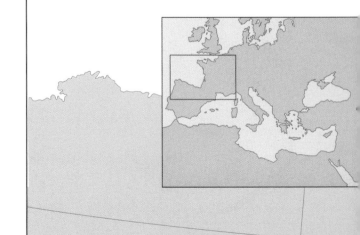

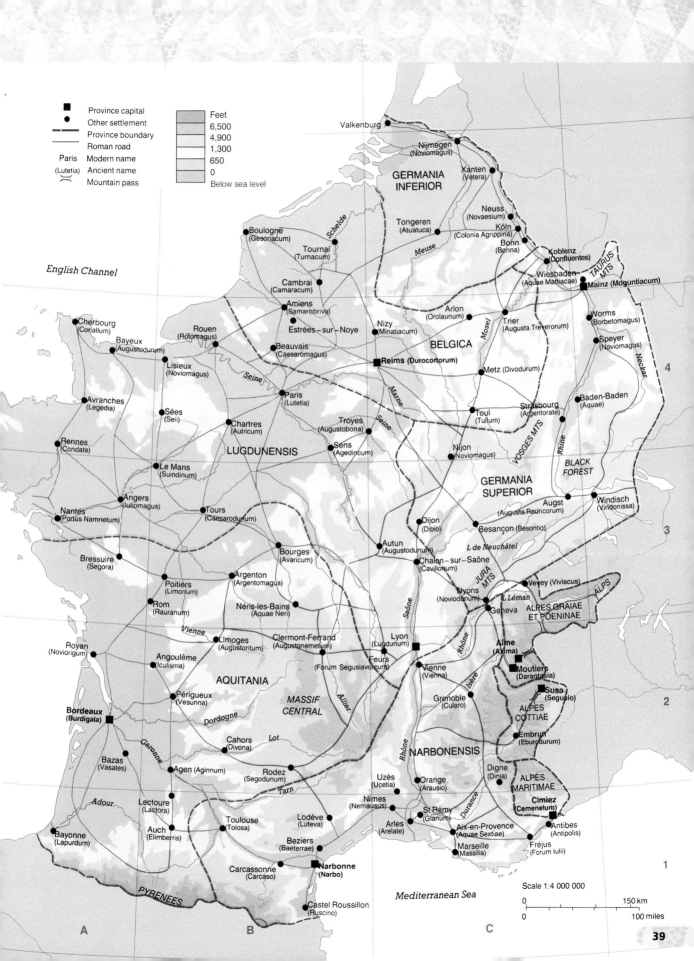

Legend

- ■ Province capital
- ● Other settlement
- --- Province boundary
- — Roman road
- Paris Modern name
- (Lutetia) Ancient name
- ‿ Mountain pass

Feet
- 6,500
- 4,900
- 1,300
- 650
- 0
- Below sea level

English Channel

Valkenburg

Nijmegen
(Noviomagus)

Xanten
(Vetera)

GERMANIA INFERIOR

Neuss
(Novaesium)

Köln
(Colonia Agrippina)

Bonn
(Bonna)

Koblenz
(Confluentes)

Tongeren
(Atuatuca)

Boulogne
(Gesoriacum)

Tournai
(Turnacum)

Schelde

Meuse

Wiesbaden
(Aquae Mattiacae)

TAURUS MTS

Mainz (Moguntiacum)

Cambrai
(Camaracum)

Amiens
(Samarobriva)

Estrées–sur–Noye

Nizy
(Minatiacum)

Arlon
(Orolaunum)

Trier
(Augusta Treverorum)

BELGICA

Worms
(Borbetomagus)

Speyer
(Noviomagus)

Cherbourg
(Coriallum)

Bayeux
(Augustodurum)

Rouen
(Rotomagus)

Beauvais
(Caesaromagus)

Lisieux
(Noviomagus)

Reims (Durocortorum)

Metz (Divodurum)

Mosel

Toul
(Tullum)

Strasbourg
(Argentorate)

Baden-Baden
(Aquae)

Avranches
(Legedia)

Sées
(Seii)

Paris
(Lutetia)

Seine

Chartres
(Autricum)

Troyes
(Augustobona)

Seine

Marne

Nijon
(Noviomagus)

VOSGES MTS

Rhine

BLACK FOREST

Rennes
(Condate)

Le Mans
(Suindinum)

LUGDUNENSIS

Sens
(Agedincum)

GERMANIA SUPERIOR

Augst
(Augusta Rauricorum)

Windisch
(Vindonissa)

Angers
(Iuliomagus)

Tours
(Caesarodunum)

Nantes
(Portus Namnetum)

Bourges
(Avaricum)

Dijon
(Dibio)

Besançon (Bésontio)

L de Neuchâtel

Bressuire
(Segora)

Argenton
(Argentomagus)

Autun
(Augustodunum)

Chalon–sur–Saône
(Cavillonum)

JURA MTS

Vevey (Viviscus)

ALPS

Poitiers
(Limonum)

Néris-les-Bains
(Aquae Neri)

Nyons
(Noviodunum)

L Léman

Geneva

ALPES GRAIAE ET POENINAE

Rom
(Rauranum)

Vienne

Saône

Rhône

Royan
(Noviorigum)

Limoges
(Augustoritum)

Clermont-Ferrand
(Augustonemetum)

Lyon
(Lugdunum)

Aîme
(Axima)

Angoulême
(Iculisma)

Feurs
(Forum Segusiavorum)

Vienne
(Vienna)

Isère

Moutiers
(Darantasia)

Susa
(Segusio)

AQUITANIA

MASSIF CENTRAL

Allier

Grenoble
(Cularo)

ALPES COTTIAE

Périgueux
(Vesunna)

Bordeaux
(Burdigala)

Dordogne

Cahors
(Divona)

Lot

Embrun
(Eburodurum)

Bazas
(Vasates)

Garonne

Agen (Aginnum)

Rodez
(Segodunum)

Tarn

Uzès
(Ucetia)

Orange
(Arausio)

Digne
(Dinia)

ALPES MARITIMAE

NARBONENSIS

Rhône

Durance

Cimiez
(Cemenelum)

Lectoure
(Lactora)

Adour

Toulouse
(Tolosa)

Lodève
(Luteva)

Nîmes
(Nemausus)

St Rémy
(Glanum)

Aix-en-Provence
(Aquae Sextiae)

Antibes
(Antipolis)

Bayonne
(Lapurdum)

Auch
(Elimberris)

Béziers
(Baeterrae)

Arles
(Arelate)

Marseille
(Massilia)

Fréjus
(Forum Iulii)

Carcassonne
(Carcaso)

Narbonne
(Narbo)

PYRENEES

Castel Roussillon
(Ruscino)

Mediterranean Sea

Scale 1:4 000 000

0 — 150 km

0 — 100 miles

A   B   C

Estrées-sur-Noye

Archeologists have surveyed a region in northern France close to the Somme River. Archeologists believe that during the Roman Empire the  land was fertile and well farmed. Air and land surveys have revealed the presence of more than 1,000 villas. The villa, or farming estate, at Estrées-sur-Noye in the valley of the Somme River was typical of the villas in the region. It is close to the town of Amiens, which the Romans called Samarobriva, in the province of Gallia.

This Roman villa was constructed within a walled courtyard that measured 385 yards (350 m) in length. As well as the owner's house, there were a number of cottages or dormitories for the farm workers within the compound.

Trier

The people who lived in the north-eastern part of Gaul were known as the Treveri. When Emperor Augustus visited the provinces in Gaul, he created a new city at Trier in 15–13 BCE and called it Augusta Treverorum (a name which means "the city of the Treveri people founded by Augustus"). Much later, Emperor Constantine lived in Trier and built a cathedral or basilica for Christian worship. He also built the largest public baths anywhere outside Rome itself, as well as a palace and a great basilica, called the Palastaula, which is known today as the Constantine Basilica.

In 326 CE, parts of the imperial family's private residential palaces were expanded and Trier became an important seat of government for the western Roman Empire. However, in the 5th century CE, Trier declined after barbarians repeatedly attacked it.

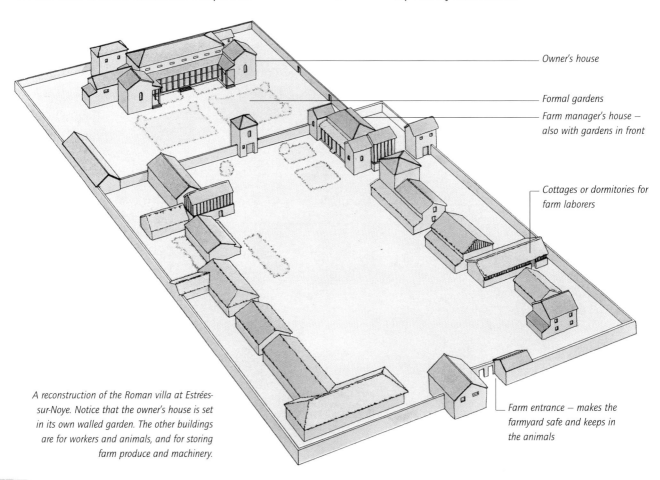

Owner's house

Formal gardens

Farm manager's house – also with gardens in front

Cottages or dormitories for farm laborers

Farm entrance – makes the farmyard safe and keeps in the animals

A reconstruction of the Roman villa at Estrées-sur-Noye. Notice that the owner's house is set in its own walled garden. The other buildings are for workers and animals, and for storing farm produce and machinery.

Nîmes

Beneath the modern city of Nîmes in southern France lie the ruins of the Roman city of Nemausus. Before it became a Roman town, Nemausus was originally a Celtic and later a Greek settlement. It became a colony of Roman citizens during Emperor Augustus's rule. The Roman city was laid out in 16 BCE and was originally intended as a home for retired soldiers. The city lay on a strategically important road that linked Italy to Spain, and, as such, it was one of the most populated and important urban centers in southern Gaul. However, its wealth came not from trade but from the export of its quality farming produce to Rome and elsewhere.

As a result of its role as a farming center, the city grew very wealthy. By the second

This aqueduct, called Pont du Gard, was built in the time of the Emperor Augustus to carry water to the city of Nemausus in Gaul from a source 30 miles (48 km) away. The remains of Nemausus lie beneath the modern city of Nîmes in France.

century CE, Nemausus had a population of around 50,000 people. It enhanced its reputation further when it produced a Roman emperor in the second century, with Emperor Antoninus Pius.

Today, the city is famous for its well-preserved Roman remains, including the amphitheater, the spectacular Pont du Gard (an aqueduct), and a temple known as Maison Carrée. Nemausus was also home to a complex of baths and pools that were fed with water from the sacred spring of the god Nemausus, from whom the city took its name.

BRITAIN

Emperor Julius Caesar was fascinated by Britain and he wrote of it in his book *The War in Gaul*: "The population is very large, and there are very many farmhouses similar to those the Gauls build. There are a large number of cattle. For coins, they use bronze or gold or iron bars. Tin is found inland, and small quantities of iron near the coast. There is also timber of every kind. All the Britons ... wear their hair long, and the men have moustaches."

Caesar wanted to conquer Britain partly to stop Celtic troublemakers from fleeing from Gaul across the English Channel to Britain, where they could find a safe haven and could plan further rebellions against Rome. Another one of Britain's attractions was its abundance of natural resources. All of the Roman provinces had to contribute to the coffers of Rome, and, as well as its plentiful sources of metals, Britain had other valuable potential exports, such as leather, hunting dogs, and a supply of slaves. The people of Britain also grew corn, which could be used feed the Roman legions stationed along the River Rhine.

A series of invasions

Julius Caesar invaded Britain twice—in 55 BCE and in 54 BCE—but he did not station any of his troops there permanently. When Emperor Claudius turned his attention to Britain a century later, he saw it as a good opportunity to prove his military worth. In 43 CE, Claudius

The Roman army built two permanent northern frontiers in Britain. The Emperor Hadrian established the stone wall that bears his name, with its series of forts. Not many years later, the Emperor Antoninus built a turf wall farther north.

traveled to Britain to join his army of 40,000 soldiers. They had just fought their way north from the south coast of Britain up to the River Thames. Claudius then led a triumphal procession with elephants to take possession of the capital of ancient Britain, known as Camulodunum (the present-day town of Colchester) in south-eastern England.

"Romanization" and prosperity

However, Emperor Claudius only stayed for 16 days in Britain. Aulus Plautius, the Roman army commander, remained behind in Britain as its first provincial governor. He then set about the task of expanding Roman territory in Britain, first in the southwest.

The Romans gradually took control of most of England and Wales, building roads and forts as they went. However, the Romans failed to conquer Scotland and so they built a defensive wall—Hadrian's Wall, named for Emperor Hadrian, who had it built in 122 CE—to keep the Celts at bay. When it was completed in around 128 CE, the wall was 73 miles (117 km) long with forts along its length, where garrisons were stationed. Further north, the Antonine Wall formed the northernmost limit of the empire

With the exception of the mountainous regions of Wales and Scotland, the rest of Britain fell to the Romans. The road network spread and towns started to grow around the sites of army garrisons. As elsewhere, army veterans and their families also established colonies, and intermarriage between Romans and Britons took place. The wealthy lived in large villas in the countryside.

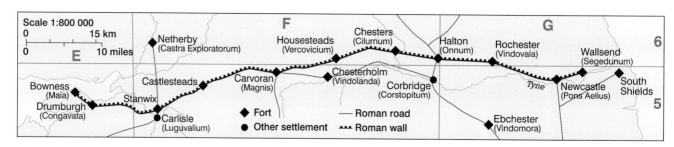

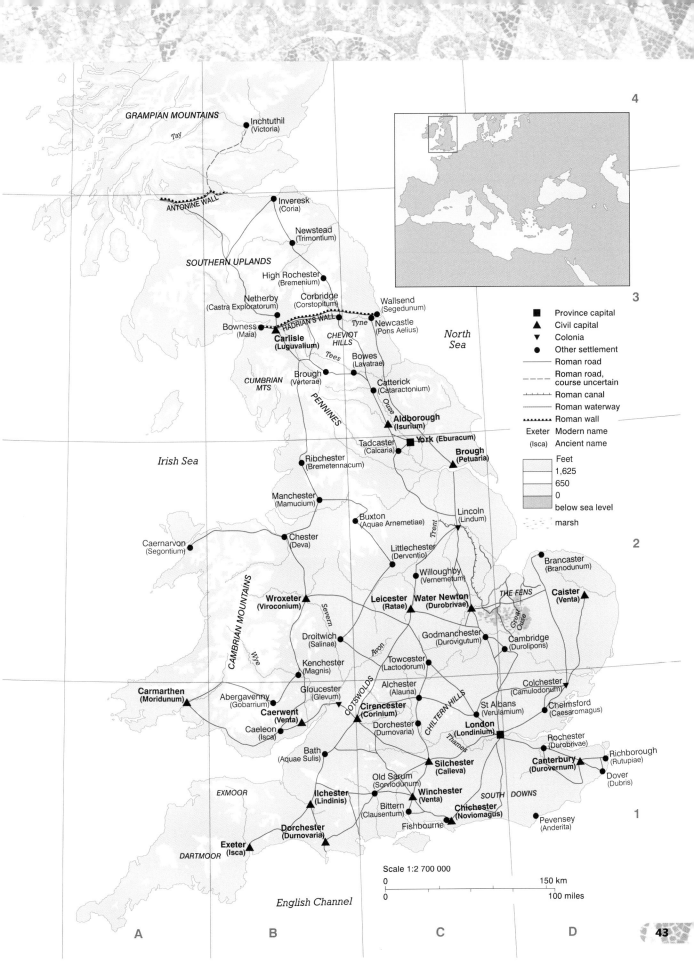

GRAMPIAN MOUNTAINS

Inchtuthil
(Victoria)

Tay

ANTONINE WALL

Inveresk
(Coria)

Newstead
(Trimontium)

SOUTHERN UPLANDS

High Rochester
(Bremenium)

Netherby
(Castra Exploratorum)

Corbridge
(Corstopitum)

HADRIAN'S WALL

Wallsend
(Segedunum)

Bowness
(Maia)

Carlisle
(Luguvalium)

Tyne

Newcastle
(Pons Aelius)

CHEVIOT
HILLS

North
Sea

CUMBRIAN
MTS

Brough
(Verterae)

Tees

Bowes
(Lavatrae)

Catterick
(Cataractonium)

PENNINES

Ouse

Aldborough
(Isurium)

Ribchester
(Bremetennacum)

Tadcaster
(Calcaria)

York (Eburacum)

Brough
(Petuaria)

Irish Sea

Manchester
(Mamucium)

Buxton
(Aquae Arnemetiae)

Lincoln
(Lindum)

Brancaster
(Branodunum)

Caernarvon
(Segontium)

Chester
(Deva)

Littlechester
(Derventio)

Trent

THE FENS

Caister
(Venta)

CAMBRIAN MOUNTAINS

Wroxeter
(Viroconium)

Willoughby
(Vernemetum)

Leicester
(Ratae)

Water Newton
(Durobrivae)

Great
Ouse

Droitwich
(Salinae)

Severn

Godmanchester
(Durovigutum)

Cambridge
(Durolipons)

Kenchester
(Magnis)

Avon

Towcester
(Lactodorum)

Wye

Carmarthen
(Moridunum)

Abergavenny
(Gobarrium)

Gloucester
(Glevum)

COTSWOLDS

Alchester
(Alauna)

Colchester
(Camulodunum)

Caerwent
(Venta)

Cirencester
(Corinium)

CHILTERN HILLS

St Albans
(Verulamium)

Chelmsford
(Caesaromagus)

Caeleon
(Isca)

Dorchester
(Durnovaria)

London
(Londinium)

Rochester
(Durobrivae)

Bath
(Aquae Sulis)

Thames

Richborough
(Rutupiae)

Silchester
(Calleva)

Canterbury
(Durovernum)

EXMOOR

Old Sarum
(Sorviodunum)

Winchester
(Venta)

Dover
(Dubris)

Ilchester
(Lindinis)

Bittern
(Clausentum)

SOUTH   DOWNS

Chichester
(Noviomagus)

Dorchester
(Durnovaria)

Fishbourne

Pevensey
(Anderita)

Exeter
(Isca)

DARTMOOR

English Channel

Scale 1:2 700 000

0		150 km
0		100 miles

■ Province capital
▲ Civil capital
▼ Colonia
● Other settlement
— Roman road
--- Roman road, course uncertain
+++ Roman canal
— Roman waterway
···· Roman wall
Exeter Modern name
(Isca) Ancient name

Feet
1,625
650
0
below sea level
marsh

4

3

2

1

A   B   C   D   **43**

Silchester

The many towns that were established in the Roman province of Britain had different origins. Some grew up around the site of an army camp or fort, while others were set up as colonies for retired soldiers who had served in Britain. The Romans also encouraged the local people to turn their own settlements into towns based on the Roman model and to adapt Roman ways of life.

In the southern county of Hampshire, the Atrebates tribe settled at a place the Romans called "Calleva Atrebatum" (which means "the town in the woods of the Atrebates"). This settlement, today known as Silchester, became the capital of the region under Roman rule.

Calleva was well located, as it stood on a crossroads of major communications routes in southern Britain. The town was laid out along the typical Roman grid pattern, with straight streets crossing at right angles splitting the settlement into regularly sized blocks. The original settlement was replaced around 200 CE with stone buildings.

The town had the usual Roman public buildings, partly for the convenience of Roman citizens but also in order to encourage the local people to begin adopting the Roman way of life. The forum lay at the heart of the town, where the main streets intersected. Around 3,000 people probably lived in the town at its height. Calleva had public baths and temples, and, although there was no theater, there was an amphitheater outside the city walls for staging sports contests and other events.

The remains of the city walls still stand at Silchester. The walls, were built in the third century CE to defend the settlement from attack. They were constructed from flint and mortar, with layers of stone included for additional strength.

Hadrian's Wall

Continuing raids and attacks by different local tribes meant that the Romans always needed a large military presence in Britain. In addition, Emperor Hadrian (ruled 117–138 CE) ordered the building of a stone wall to provide a defensive barrier to protect the province from the aggressive peoples of the far north. The wall extended from the east to the west coast of northern Britain for a distance of 73 miles (117 km), running from Segedunum (present-day Wallsend) in the east to Bowness on the Solway Firth in the west.

The initial construction took six years and the wall was added to at later dates. The original plan was to build a wall more than

Hadrian's Wall in Britain was commissioned by the Roman emperor Hadrian in the second century CE. It was constructed to keep the tribes of present-day Scotland from encroaching south into the Roman province of Britain. The wall was 73 miles (117 km) long.

10 feet (3.3 m) wide and at least 12 feet (4m) high in the eastern sector, and with a 20-foot (6-m) wide turf rampart base along the western end. The finished wall had frequent watch towers and forts spaced at roughly 7-mile (11 km) intervals. The wall was built by soldiers from the three legions serving in Britain and when completed it was slightly lower and narrower than the original plan. Today, large segments of the wall survive.

THE DANUBE

This region was the military backbone of the Roman Empire for two reasons. Firstly, Its geographical location meant that the "front-line" states of the provinces of Germany and those to the south of the Danube River buffered the rest of the empire, sitting to the west, from warring tribes in the north. The Romans called those tribes *barbari* (barbarians), because they felt the word copied the tribes' speech. The barbarians did not speak Latin or live like the Romans. Secondly, the provinces of the Danube were a source of recruits for the Roman legions. The recruits were men from towns or the countryside who, in the third and fourth centuries CE, often rose to become Roman officers

Natural frontier

The River Danube was a natural frontier, but the Romans did not like to rely on it entirely for protection. Instead, they built a number of legionary forts along its the southern banks. The Romans considered the area between the Rhine and Danube rivers a potentially weak

point in their northern defenses. To protect it, they built a permanent barrier with a patrol road, known as the *limes*. The defenses were erected to guard against invasion by Germanic peoples who lived to the north. Over a length of 350 miles (550 km) from the Rhine in the northwest to the Danube in the southeast, the *limes* consisted of a series of watchtowers, forts, ditches, ramparts, and stone walls. The Black Sea provided another natural barrier at the Roman Empire's north-eastern boundary.

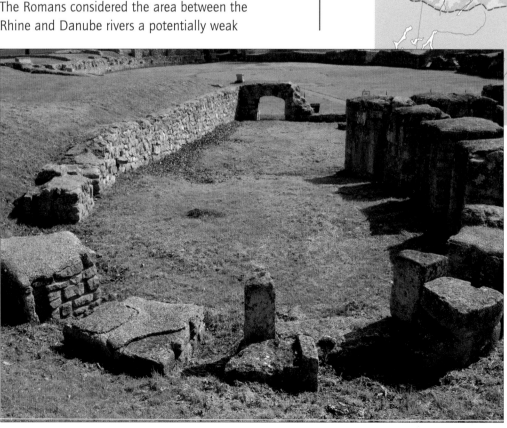

The earth-and-stone amphitheater at Carnutum, near modern Vienna on the Danube River in Austria, could hold up to 13,000 spectators.

Meanwhile, the Romans continued to expand their growing empire. By 106 CE, the Roman army had conquered the new province of Dacia (now part of the modern-day country of Romania). Here, the Romans built a number of new towns and colonies, in many cases for the purpose of housing retired army veterans and their families. The depth of Roman the influence in Dacia in a relatively short period of 150 years can be seen in the similarities of the modern Romanian language and Latin.

Growth of towns

Across the Danube region, Roman towns grew up at legionary forts, as traders and families of Roman soldiers settled there. Small villages, called *canabae*, developed into larger towns.

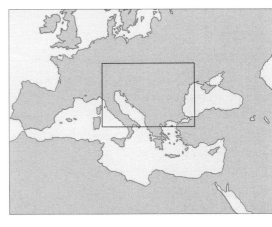

The Danube region of the Roman Empire, stretched from present-day Germany in the north right down to the Black Sea in the south-east.

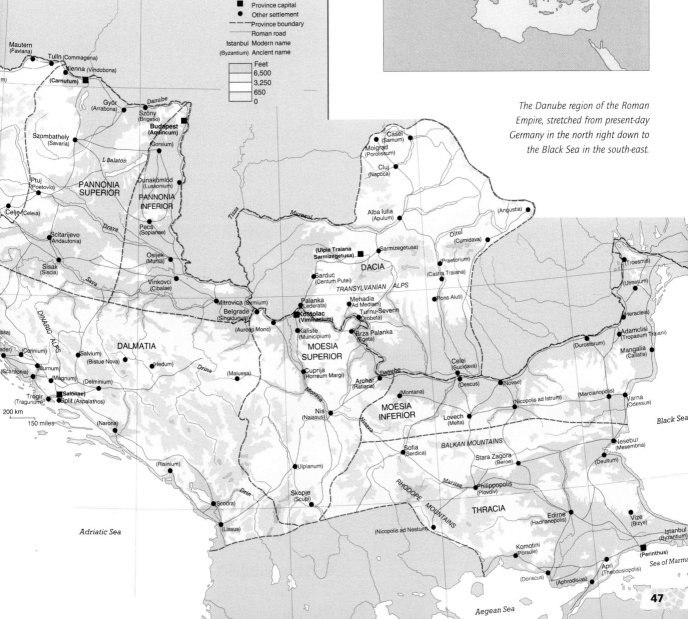

GREECE AND THE BALKANS

The first Roman "university professor" was called Quintilian. He was a great admirer of the Greeks, as were many Romans. Based in Athens, in Greece, Quintilian was also the tutor of Emperor Vespasian's children. It was quite normal for rich Romans to send their sons—but not their daughters—to Athens to finish their schooling.

Quintilian spoke for many Romans when he said, "I prefer that a boy should learn Greek as his first language. He will soon pick up Latin, whether he likes it or not, as it is in general use. At the same time, he ought first to be instructed in Greek learning, from which ours is derived."

The Roman conquest of Greece came at the conclusion of a lengthy and complex military, diplomatic, and commercial involvement by the Romans in Greece. The provinces that were finally created by the Romans differed greatly in character to those ruled by the Greeks. Under Roman rule, some parts of Greece prospered more under the Romans, with some Greek families becoming even wealthier.

Three provinces of Greece

Under Roman rule, the southern Balkan region was divided into three provinces, each with its own governor. Achaea in the south remained the center of the old Greek civilization. The Romans oversaw the restoration and rebuilding of several of its cities and sacred places, including Delphi, home to the famous Oracle.

A great deal of restoration work took place during the second century CE. A rich Athenian, Herodes Atticus, paid for much of the building work, which included a theater in Athens, an aqueduct at Olympia, healing pools for the sick at Thermoplylae, and a stadium at Delphi.

In the north, Thessalonica (present-day Saloniki) became the provincial capital of Macedonia. As well as being an important port, it became a Roman colony in the middle of the third century CE. In the fifth century CE, Thessalonica was enlarged when town walls, the church St Demetrius, and a new prefect's palace were built.

Early Christianity

Greece under Roman rule is a period closely associated with Christianity, as accounts in the Bible tell. St Paul traveled to Greece on his second journey. He was arrested in the Roman colony of Philippi following a riot, and he was only released when the authorities realized he was a Roman citizen. Paul would later preach the Christian message in Athens and Corinth.

Sightseers look out over the modern city of Thessalonica in northern Greece from the ruins of the massive Roman walls built to protect the ancient settlement in the fifth century CE.

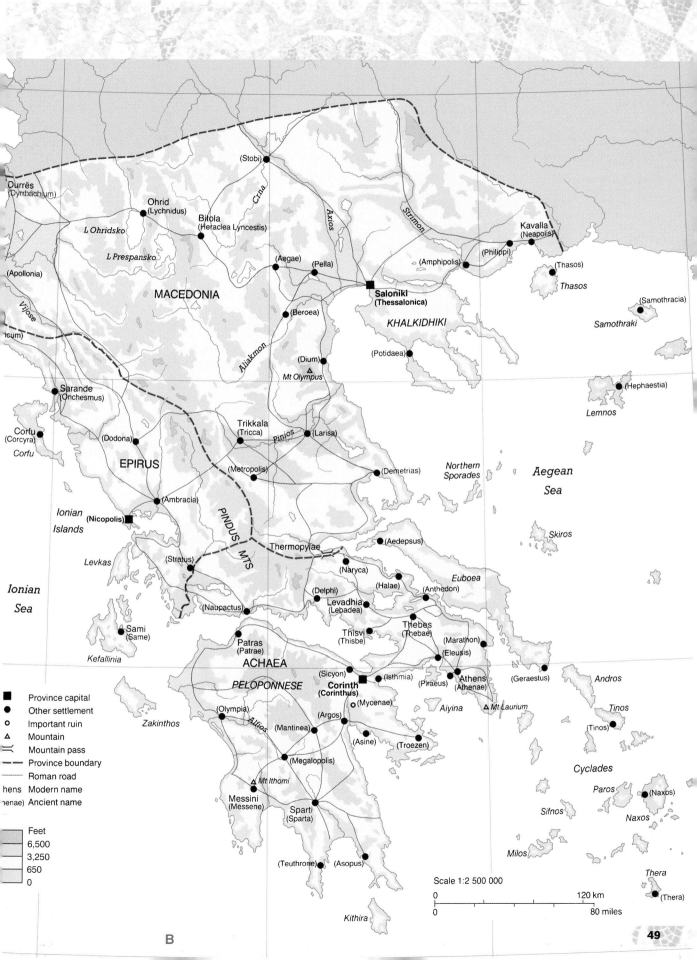

Durrës
(Dyrrhachium)

(Stobi)

Ohrid
(Lychnidus)

Crna

L Ohridsko

Bitola
(Heraclea Lyncestis)

L Prespansko

Axios

(Apollonia)

(Aegae)   (Pella)

Strimon

Kavalla
(Neapolis)

(Amphipolis)

(Philippi)

(Thasos)

MACEDONIA

Saloniki
(Thessalonica)

Thasos

Vijose

(Beroea)

KHALKIDHIKI

(Samothracia)

icum)

Aliakmon

(Dium)

△
Mt Olympus

(Potidaea)

Samothraki

Sarande
(Onchesmus)

(Hephaestia)

Lemnos

Corfu
(Corcyra)

(Dodona)

Trikkala
(Tricca)

Pinios (Larisa)

Northern
Sporades

Aegean
Sea

Corfu

EPIRUS

(Metropolis)

(Demetrias)

Ionian
Islands

(Nicopolis) ■

(Ambracia)

Skiros

(Aedepsus)

Thermopylae

Levkas

(Stratus)

P
I
N
D
U
S

M
T
S

(Naryca)

Euboea

(Halae)

(Anthedon)

Ionian
Sea

(Naupactus)

(Delphi)

Levadhia
(Lebadea)

Thebes
(Thebae)

Sami
(Same)

Thisvi
(Thisbe)

(Marathon)

Kefallinia

Patras
(Patrae)

(Eleusis)

ACHAEA

(Sicyon)

(Isthmia)

Athens
(Athenae)

(Geraestus)

Andros

PELOPONNESE

Corinth
(Corinthus)

■

(Piraeus)

■ Province capital

● Other settlement

○ Important ruin

(Mycenae) ○

Aiyina

△ *Mt Laurium*

Tinos

(Olympia)

Alfios

(Argos)

Zakinthos

Mantinea

(Asine)

(Tinos)

△ Mountain

≍ Mountain pass

(Troezen)

(Megalopolis)

Cyclades

▬ ▬ Province boundary

Roman road

hens Modern name

nae) Ancient name

△ *Mt Ithomi*

Messini
(Messene)

Sparti
(Sparta)

Paros

(Naxos)

Feet

6,500

Sifnos

Naxos

3,250

(Teuthrone) (Asopus)

Milos

650

0

Scale 1:2 500 000

Thera

(Thera)

0   120 km

0   80 miles

Kithira

Athens

During the early days of the Roman Empire, the Romans destroyed much of the ancient city of Athens, one of the most eminent and powerful city-states of ancient Greece. In the first century BCE, for example, the armies of the consul Sulla destroyed many ancient buildings and monuments. However, later Roman emperors undertook massive building programs in the city. Julius Caesar and Augustus both erected prominent public buildings, while Emperor Hadrian also carried out a number of public works. Under the Roman Empire, wealthy Athenians also constructed new buildings in their city. Herodes Atticus, for example, built a concert theater (*odeum*) that could hold more than 5,000 people.

Emperor Hadrian in Athens

Hadrian visited Athens for the first time in 124–25 CE. By the end of his reign in 138 CE, Hadrian had changed the city almost beyond recognition. He finished a large temple to the Greek god Zeus (the Romans called him Jupiter) begun in the sixth century BCE. He spent three winters in Athens and oversaw the completion there of an aqueduct, a gymnasium, a large library, and a bridge. In addition to these projects, Hadrian ordered the construction of a temple dedicated to all Greeks.

Hadrian also built a triumphal arch on a street that led from the old city of Athens to the new Roman city. There are two inscriptions on the arch. On the side leading to the old city it reads, "This is Athens, the ancient city of Theseus", and on the other, "This is the city of Hadrian and not of Theseus"!

Inside the first-century-BCE "Tower of the Winds" in Athens, Greece, was a 24-hour clock driven by water power. The exterior of the building is decorated with wall sculptures showing the "eight winds." It was originally topped with a weathervane.

Corinth

Corinth was one of the most spectacular cities of ancient Greece. After its citizens tried unsuccessfully to fight the Romans in the second century BCE, the city was destroyed. Corinth was set on fire, its people made slaves, and its treasures looted by command of the Roman consul Lucius Mummius.

Over a century later, Julius Caesar chose the site of the destroyed city to become a colony for retired soldiers. He ordered the reconstruction of ruined buildings and planned a new city. Roman Corinth became a major trading and business center, quickly recovering its prosperity. It was also chosen as the seat of government for the Roman province of Achaea.

Restoring the Greek city

Rising above every other building in Corinth was the temple to the Greek god Apollo. The temple

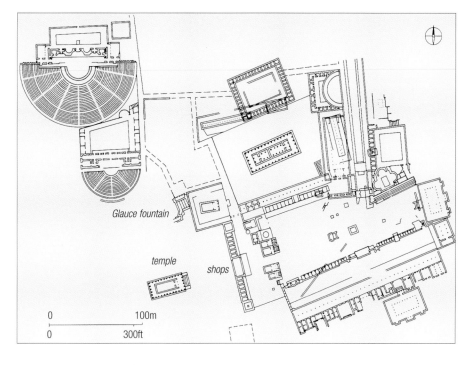

Plan of Roman Corinth. The Romans added a number of temples to the city center.

Glauce fountain

temple

shops

0   100m

0   300ft

originally dated from the sixth century BCE and the Romans restored it. Other structures included a triumphal arch through which was the main entry to the city from the harbor. The forum, as was typical of all Roman towns, was the business area. Its importance was reflected in the magnificent buildings that surrounded it.

Other important buildings included the basilicas, used for meetings and law courts. Since Corinth was the capital of Greece during Roman times, there was a lot of administratve paperwork to get through.

Herodes Atticus paid for another theater here. Cut into rock, the small theater could seat up to 3,000. He also rebuilt an elaborate public fountain in the center of the city. Corinth was destroyed for a second time in 521 CE, this time by an earthquake.

The Corinth canal

One of the most spectacular sights of modern Greece is the canal that links the Gulf of Corinth to the Aegean Sea. The Corinth Canal was finished in 1893, but it was the Roman emperors who began the project 2,000 years before. Caligula surveyed the ground and Nero ordered 6,000 Jewish slaves to begin digging the ground in 67 CE.

Only a few columns still stand of the famous temple of Apollo at Corinth. The temple was built by the Greeks in the sixth century BCE but was later restored by the Romans.

ASIA MINOR

During the reign of the Seleucid king Antiochus III, who ruled the Hellenistic Syrian Empire from 223–187 BCE, the Romans turned their attention to the Asia Minor region. The Romans defeated Antiochus in a number of battles in 190 BCE and three other kings gave

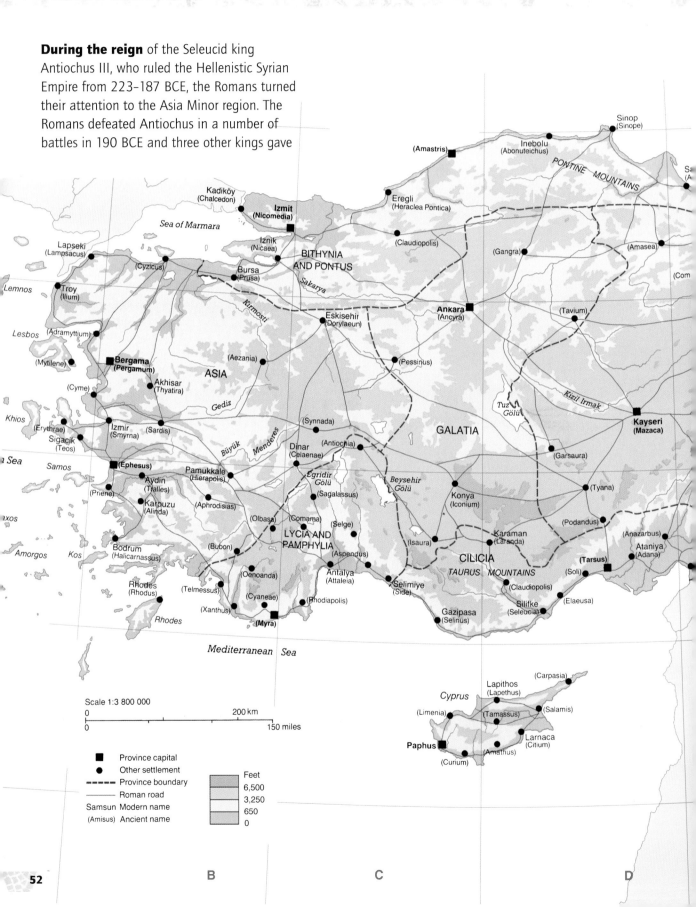

Sinop
(Sinope)

(Amastris)

Inebolu
(Abonuteichus)

PONTINE MOUNTAINS

Sa

(Sa

Kadıköy
(Chalcedon)

Eregli
(Heraclea Pontica)

İzmit
(Nicomedia)

Sea of Marmara

İznik
(Nicaea)

(Claudiopolis)

(Amasea)

Lapseki
(Lampsacus)

BITHYNIA
AND PONTUS

(Cyzicus)

Bursa
(Prusa)

(Gangra)

(Com

Lemnos

Troy
(Ilium)

Sakarya

Kırmostı

Eskisehir
(Dorylaeun)

Ankara
(Ancyra)

(Tavium)

Lesbos

(Adramyttium)

(Aezania)

(Pessinus)

(Mytilene)

Bergama
(Pergamum)

ASIA

Akhisar
(Thyatira)

Tuz
Gölü

Kızıl Irmak

Khios

(Erythrae)

Gediz

GALATIA

Kayseri
(Mazaca)

Sığacık
(Teos)

İzmir
(Smyrna)

(Sardis)

(Synnada)

Büyük   Menderes

Dinar
(Celaenae)

(Antiochia)

(Garsaura)

a Sea

Samos

(Ephesus)

Pamukkale
(Hierapolis)

Egridir
Gölü

Beyşehir
Gölü

Konya
(Iconium)

(Tyana)

(Priene)

Aydın
(Tralles)

(Sagalassus)

axos

Karpuzu
(Alinda)

(Aphrodisias)

(Olbasa)

(Comama)

(Selge)

(Podandus)

(Anazarbus)

Bodrum
(Halicarnassus)

(Bubon)

LYCIA AND
PAMPHYLIA

(Aspendus)

(Isaura)

Karaman
(Laranda)

CILICIA

(Tarsus)

Ataniya
(Adana)

Amorgos

Kos

(Oenoanda)

Antalya
(Attaleia)

TAURUS   MOUNTAINS

(Soli)

Rhodes
(Rhodus)

(Telmessus)

(Cyaneae)

(Rhodiapolis)

Selimiye
(Side)

(Claudiopolis)

Silifke
(Seleucia)

(Elaeusa)

(Xanthus)

(Myra)

Gazipasa
(Selinus)

Rhodes

Mediterranean   Sea

(Carpasia)

Lapithos
(Lapethus)

Cyprus

(Limenia)

Tamassus

(Salamis)

Paphus

Larnaca
(Citium)

Amathus

(Curium)

Scale 1:3 800 000

0   200 km

0   150 miles

■   Province capital
●   Other settlement
---- Province boundary
──   Roman road
Samsun Modern name
(Amisus) Ancient name

Feet
6,500
3,250
650
0

B   C   D

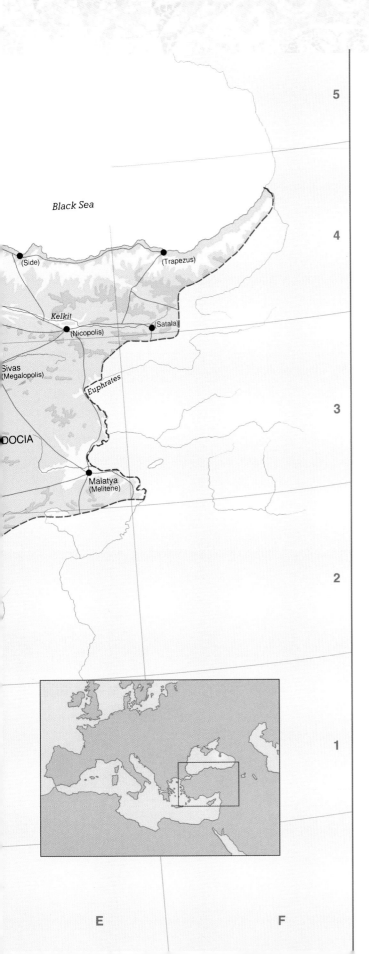

Black Sea

(Side)

(Trapezus)

Kelkit

(Nicopolis)

(Satala)

Sivas
(Megalopolis)

Euphrates

DOCIA

Malatya
(Melitene)

5

4

3

2

1

E   F

the Romans their territory. Only two regions—Lycia and Cilicia—remained for the Romans to conquer. These regions, located on the Anatolian plateau, were populated with small villages, and the peasants who lived there were often recruited into the Roman armies.

Pirates

Pirates were a big threat in the region. Although they lived on the land, the pirates hunted down the ships that sailed the eastern Mediterranean Sea and plundered them for the trade goods and other riches that were being transported to Rome and other centers of the Roman empire. After many battles with the pirates, the Roman naval commander Pompey the Great finally succeeded in defeating the pirates in 67 BCE.

The Greeks had already established a number of important cities in Asia Minor, particularly along the coastlines, before the Romans arrived. The Romans built on and expanded the existing infrastructure of roads and set about developing new colonies. Emperor Augustus, in particular, established more Roman colonies in Asia Minor than any other emperor. These colonies included those at Antiochia, Olbasa, and Iconium.

Roman Cyprus

The Mediterranean island of Cyprus belonged to Egypt for almost 250 years before it became part of the Roman Empire in 58 BCE. Its capital city was Paphus, but the port of Salamis became the islands' biggest city and trading center.

Some Romans became very rich from trading in Cyprus's many exports, which included timber, copper, and corn. Though the merchants grew rich, the island suffered as a result of the exploitation of these raw materials. The territory converted to Christianity after the apostle Paul visited in 45 CE.

The Roman conquest of Asia Minor saw the region divided up into provinces, where many existing Greek settlements were developed into Roman towns and cities. The Romans improved the roads and used them to export goods to the rest of the empire.

Ephesus

The city of Ephesus became the capital of the new Roman province of Asia after King Attalus III left his kingdom to the Romans in his will in

133 BCE. The city already had an illustrious past. Under the Greeks, it was a rich town famous for its temple, one of the Seven Wonders of the Ancient World, dedicated to the goddess Artemis. Ephesus was an important port (today, the coastline of Turkey has moved and the city is no longer on the shore) and, during the Greek

The statue of the goddess Arete, a personification of goodness and excellence, stands between two columns in the facade of the Celsus library at Ephesus. Built in the second century CE, the library held 12,000 scrolls.

period, a wall encircled the city and connected it to the harbor and the coast. As in Corinth, an impressive colonnaded street ran from the harbor to the theater. The theater had originally been constructed in the third century BCE but was rebuilt by the Romans. The rebuilding began in 41 CE and, when it was completed in around 120 CE, the theater could hold 25,000 spectators. Another important building was the library, built in honor of Celsus, a governor during the second century CE.

Much of our knowledge about Ephesus in Roman times comes not just from the large number of archeological remains that have been uncovered, but also from inscriptions. These inscriptions often describe the generosity of the leading families of the town and its rivalry with Smyrna to be the "first city" of Asia.

Aphrodisias

Saint Paul in Ephesus

The city of Ephesus is closely associated with the Christian teachings of the evangelist Saint Paul. When Paul visited, however, he caused a riot. Local silversmiths were particularly upset by his teachings, fearing that the introduction of Christianity might bring an end to their profitable business of making ornate silver offerings that people bought for the goddess Artemis. The local people were followers of Artemis and declared their loyalty to her during a heated gathering. One silversmith named Demetrius addressed a huge crowd who assembled in the city's theater. On behalf of his colleagues, Demetrius complained of the disrespect being displayed toward Artemis by Paul's Christian teaching. After this incident, Paul had to leave Ephesus for Greece.

Named after the Greek goddess of love and beauty, Aphrodite, (the Romans called her Venus), in the first century BCE, the city of Aphrodisias was very popular with important Roman figures. Generals such as Sulla and Julius Caesar and emperors such as Augustus and Hadrian often visited.

The temple of Aphrodite was built here in the first century BCE, and Emperor Hadrian added a special courtyard to it during the second century CE. Like many other Greek and Roman temples, Aphrodite's temple became a Christian church in the sixth century. The construction of such fine buildings was made possible because of the availability of fine-quality marble, which was mined close by. Many artists worked in the town and their work, especially their stone carving, had a high reputation across the empire. Marble from Aphrodisias was later exported to other parts of the Roman empire for use in many prestigious building projects.

City entertainments

Popular public entertainments changed over the course of time. In the second century CE, the theater in Aphrodisias was converted into an amphitheater for gladiatorial and wild-beast shows. The odeum, where concerts and recitals were held, was located in front of the temple of Aphrodite. The city also boasted a stadium for athletics and chariot-racing, and Emperor Hadrian built a very large bath block for the use of the town's population.

Around 265 CE, a great wall was built around most of the city to protect it against invasion by the Goths. The city continued to flourish during the late Roman period.

This carved marble panel comes from a marble tomb that now stands in the grounds of the musuem at Aphrodisias. The city was famous throughout the Roman world not just for the quality of its marble, which was widely exported, but also as a center of outstanding artistic creativity. The carvers combined elements from both the Roman and Greek styles.

THE EXOTIC EAST

The eastern provinces of the Roman Empire were originally ruled by a number of kings. The Romans made treaties with them and then they began to take over the governing of the region. In Judaea, the Romans took partial control in 6 CE and complete control in 44 CE. However, the Jews of Judaea did not accept Roman rule and continued to rebel. Syria became Roman in 64 CE, Arabia in 106 CE, and Mesopotamia in 114 CE, expanding the Roman Empire greatly.

Keeping the Roman peace

Emperor Trajan set about ensuring the new provinces remained part of the Roman Empire. He ordered the building of fortifications along the eastern edge of Arabia and Syria. As well as a network of stone-paved roads built across the desert, forts with towers in each corner were built along the frontier. Trajan flooded the area with soldiers, sending six legions to keep order. The new roads and the presence of soldiers to keep the peace enabled trade to flourish.

Trade with the east

The east provided the Roman Empire with many types of goods, including timber, cloth, glass, and leather products. The Romans liked sweet-smelling resins and gums, such as frankincense and myrrh, which also came from the east. In addition, the port of Tyrus in the eastern Mediterranean produced a purple dye, which was highly prized in the making of clothing.

A great deal of trade came through Arabia. Camel trains brought goods across the desert, covering up to 20 miles (32 km) each day. The desert city of Palmyra in Syria was an important stop on the camel route. Trade routes reached as far east as India for spices and China for silk. The Silk Route was also used by easterners traveling west to Rome.

Wild animals

Exotic animals from the furthermost provinces of the Roman Empire were highly sought after in Rome, where they were killed for sport in public amphitheatres. The town of Hierapolis (known today as Baalbek) in northern Syria became a holding port for wild animals such as lions, tigers, and leopards. The animals were transported to Alexandria in Egypt, before being shipped to Rome. Trade with Africa for ivory and ebony also took place.

The Roman theater was built in Bostra (modern Busra in Syria) in the second century CE. The city, which became the capital of the Roman province of Arabia under the Emperor Trajan, was an important junction on caravan routes into Asia.

Samsat
(Samosata)

Euphrates

TUR ABDIN

(Antinonopolis)

Urfa
(Edessa)

■ Nusaybin
(Nisibis)

(Zeugma)

Harran
(Carrhae)

MESOPOTAMIA

(Singara)

(Alexandria ad Issum)

(Cyrrhus)

Membij
(Hierapolis)

Aleppo
(Beroea)

■ Antakya
(Antiochia)

Raqqa (Nic Horium)

Euphrates

SYRIA

(Laodicea)

Orontes

(Apamea)

Risafe
(Resapha)

Khabir

Hama
(Epiphania)

(Seriane)

Buseire
(Circesium)

Mediterranean Sea

(Raphanaea)

Homs
(Emesa)

(Palmyra)

Dura-Europus

Tripoli
(Tripolis)

(Danaba)

SYRIAN DESERT

Beirut
(Berytus)

Baalbek
(Heliopolis)

■ Province capital
● Other settlement
- - - Province boundary
Roman road
Homs   Modern name
(Emesa) Ancient name

Saida
(Sidon)

Damascus

Feet
6,500
3,250
650
0
Below sea level
- - - Seasonal river

Tyre
(Tyrus)

(Caesarea Paneas)

Sea of
Galilee

El Qanawat
(Canatha)

(Tiberias)

Nazareth
(Lejjun)

Um Qeis
(Gadara)

■ Busra
(Bostra)

esarea Maritima)

■ (Scythopolis)

Jarash
(Gerasa)

Tel Aviv-Yafo
(Joppa)

(Neapolis)

JUDAEA

(Diospolis)

Jericho

Amman
(Philadelphia)

Ascalon)

Bethlehem

Jerusalem
(Aelia Capitolina)

Gaza

(Herodion)

Hebron

(Madaba)

(Masada)

Dead
Sea

ARABIA

Beersheba
(Berosaba)

Karnak
(Characmoba)

(Nessana)

Oboda

NEGEV DESERT

The eastern provinces of the Roman Empire covered what is
today known as the Mid-East. The region provided the Romans
with a wealth of exports, and was an important staging post
on the trade routes from India and China.

(Petra)

Scale 1:3 500 000

0   120 km
0   100 miles

Elat
(Aila)

A   B   C   D

Palmyra

Palmyra looms out of the desert in eastern Syria. Sited at an important desert oasis , its name may have meant "city of palms". In the first century BCE, Palmyra was a key staging post on the Syrian–Babylonian trade route. Camels transporting goods from India, China, and Arabia passed through Palmyra, where the caravans stopped to rest before traveling on to the ports of Tyrus and Sidon.

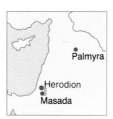

Palmyra was a target for the Romans because of its legendary wealth. In 41 BCE, soldiers led by the Roman commander Mark Antony attacked it, but failed to take control. In the early years of the empire, Palmyra remained an independent state between Rome and Parthia, but, after a visit from an envoy of Emperor Tiberius in 18 CE, the city became part of the Roman Empire. Unusually for a Roman city, Palmyra remained relatively independent because of its trading links with the east.

In the second century CE, spectacular public building projects were undertaken at Palmyra. Probably the most magnificent was the wide colonnaded street that ran across the city for almost half a mile (0.8 km). Other important buildings included the Arch of Triumph, the forum, and a huge temple dedicated to Bel, one of the most important deities worshiped in Babylonia to the east

The ruins of the oasis city of Palmyra in the Syrian desert. Palmyra was an important trade center as camel and donkey caravans would pass through on their way to and from the River Euphrates and the Persian Gulf.

Masada

Masada sits on the top of a high, rocky plateau in present-day Israel to the west of the Dead Sea. Its history as a fortress dates back 2,000 years. The Judaean king Herod developed the site into a palace-fortress to protect himself from threats from both within and outside his kingdom. After Herod's death, the site was abandoned until the siege of Masada.

The Jewish people had rebelled against foreign rule on several occasions. In 66 CE, they rose up against Roman troops stationed in Jerusalem. To suppress the uprising, Rome sent 50,000 troops to Jerusalem, which they recaptured in 70 CE. Many people were killed.

The Romans believed that they had conquered their Jewish subjects, but a group of Jews, called the Zealots, withdrew to ancient fortress in the desert, from where they continued to resist Roman rule. The Zealots had taken over the mountain fortress of Masada in 66 CE. Roman troops besieged them there for seven years. The siege was recorded by a Jewish historian called Josephus.

The remains of the ancient hilltop fortress at Masada, where a group of Jewish rebels, the Zealots, made their last stand against the Roman army in the first century CE. After a long siege, almost all the Zealots committed suicide rather than surrender to Rome.

Mountain siege

Josephus described how the commander of the Roman army, Flavius Silva, built a large ramp against the mountain so that his soldiers could attack the plateau. The Zealots knew they could not hold out indefinitely against a Roman army of 15,000, when they numbered fewer than 400. Eventually, the Zealots chose to commit suicide rather than to surrender to their attackers. They drew pottery lots to select which 10 men would be responsible for killing the other men, women, and children; the last survivor of the 10 took his own life. According to Josephus, two women and five children who hid in a water cistern were the only eyewitnesses who survived to give an account of the last days of the siege. Today Masada is a famous memorial to Jewish history.

EGYPT

Egypt was conquered first by the Greeks and then by Alexander the Great of Macedonia in 330 BCE. Alexander went on to found the city of Alexandria, which grew into a famed center of Greek learning, culture, and influence. After Alexander died in 323 BCE, a Macedonian general called Ptolemy established himself as king, and after him all Egyptian kings were called Ptolemy.

Last of the Ptolemies

From the second century BCE, the Romans began to take an interest in Egypt, and began to assert their authority there. By the first century BCE, the Romans effectively controlled the country through the Egyptian king, nicknamed Auletes ("flute player") When Auletes died, he named his daughter Cleopatra and his son Ptolemy to be his joint successors, but he also appointed Rome as their guardians, and so the Romans were now in a position to take complete control of Egypt.

In 30 BCE, after the death of Cleopatra, Emperor Augustus announced that Egypt was henceforth to be considered a Roman province. It was to be ruled by a prefect chosen by the emperor. However, Augustus and his successors treated Egypt differently from the other Roman provinces, viewing it as an imperial domain, which reflected its ancient tradition of rule

by the pharaohs and the Ptolemies. The Roman administrators therefore made no real changes to the existing system of government, except that Romans replaced Greeks as the highest officials. Unlike almost everywhere else in the Roman Empire, the Romans did not try to settle in Egypt in massive numbers, and most of the existing daily routines remained rooted in Greek culture throughout the period of Roman rule.

We know a great deal about Roman rule in Egypt, because of the many thousands of papyri documents that have been found.

Corn for Rome

Alexandria was the capital city and the main port of Egypt. During Greek rule, the city had grown into a very important center of Greek culture and influence. It was also the second largest city in the entire Roman Empire. Corn, which was a staple part of the Roman diet, was transported from Alexandria across the empire. Egypt was able to supply all the corn for its own needs, as well as for Rome because the annual flooding of the Nile River left the lands that lay along its banks very fertile and ideal for agriculture. As well as corn, Egyptian exports included papyrus for writing on (the Romans did not have paper), flax for making cloth, perfumes, medicines, olives, and dates.

Cyrenaica and Crete

Cyrenaica was a region located 500 miles (800 km) to the west of Egypt along the North African coast. It was an area that had previously been home to a collection of Greek colonies. It became a Roman

The 99-foot-tall (30-m) Pompey's Pillar rises above an ancient Egyptian sphinx in the port of Alexandria. Despite the monument's name, it was in fact erected by the Emperor Diocletian in 293. It was originally part of the front of a temple.

The modern harbor at Alexandria. In Roman times, the city was the most important port in the empire.

province in 74 BCE. Its most important city was Cyrene, which was damaged during the Jewish Revolt of 115 CE. The Roman emperor Hadrian restored the city. The Romans ruled Cyrenaica along with Crete as a single province.

The Romans had conquered the island of Crete by 67 BCE, and, under the command of Roman general Quintus Metellus and his legions, Roman rule was often very harsh, although the island was prosperous during the Roman period. The many large villas built on Crete during this time are proof of its prosperity.

This carving at Dendara in Egypt shows Cleopatra (left) with Caesarion, the son she had with Julius Caesar.

GLOSSARY

amphitheater Really means "theater in the round" because of its oval shape. This was where gladiators fought.

amphora A huge pottery jar used to transport and store olive oil, wine, and fish sauce.

aqueduct Channel that brought water into the towns and cities, sometimes raised high upon arches to cross rivers or ravines.

barbari Literally means "barbarians." The Romans used the name for anyone who was not Roman or did not speak Latin.

basilica A long building with aisles, used as a public hall mainly for ceremonies and law courts.

censor An elected official who kept a register of all Roman citizens.

centurion A soldier in charge of about 80 to 100 men in the Roman army. His rank was similar to that of a sergeant today.

colonia A town of retired soldiers and their families set up in the provinces.

consul The highest office a politician could hold in the republic. Each year two consuls shared responsibility for the government, the army, and the law courts.

curia The name given to the building where the senate met to discuss public affairs.

diocese The name given by the emperor Diocletian to his 12 areas of government throughout the empire.

emperor Imperator in Latin; this was the title adopted by the emperor Augustus. An emperor held supreme power in the Roman state.

forum Originally, the open market-place in a Roman town (the Greeks called it the agora). Most important public buildings were grouped in and around the forum.

gladiators Warriors who fought bouts to the death in the amphitheater. They wore armor of different kinds.

hypocaust The system used to heat floors and walls of buildings, mainly the baths. Hot air from a fire flowed under raised floors and through pipes in the walls.

insula Literally means "island" and was the name for a block of buildings, surrounded by streets, in a town.

Legatus The title used by the commander of a legion and the governor of a province.

legion The main unit in the Roman army. Usually made up of about 5,500 Roman citizens in the first century CE.

mosaic A floor (or sometimes a wall) made up of many fragments (called tesserae) of stone, tile, or glass. Polished smooth, it made a picture or design.

odeum A small theater used for concerts and recitals.

orator A lawyer or politician well known for making public speeches.

papyrus The Roman "paper" made from the stems of a water plant of the same name.

patricians The nobles, or upper class, of Roman society.

plebeians The name given to the ordinary working people of Roman society.

praetors The officials elected as judges in the Roman state.

procurators People appointed to look after the finances in the provinces. Some might be governors of small provinces.

provinces Areas taken over and governed by the Romans. Italy, for example, was a province of Rome.

quaestors Officials voted in to be in charge of all the state's finances—the treasury.

republic The word the Romans used for their state with its elected officials and government.

senate A large group of ex-officials who formed a type of "parliament" in Rome. They discussed public affairs and advised the elected officials such as the consuls.

thermae The Latin word for the public baths, with their sweating room (caldarium) and sauna (laconicum).

toga The outer garment (a large semicircular piece of cloth) which could only be worn by a citizen, therefore a man.

villa A farming estate as well as a house in the country or by the seaside.

FURTHER RESOURCES

PUBLICATIONS

Baker, S. Ancient Rome: *The Rise and Fall of the Empire* (BBC Books, 2007).

Connolly, P. *The Cavalryman* (Oxford University Press, 1988).

Connolly, P. *The Legionary* (Oxford University Press, 1988).

Connolly, P. *The Roman Fort* (Oxford University Press, 1991).

Corbishley, M. *Illustrated Encyclopedia of Ancient Rome* (The J. Paul Getty Museum/British Museum, 2003).

Corbishley, M. *Real Romans* (English Heritage/TAG Publishing, 1999).

Corbishley, M. *The Roman World* (Watts, 1986).

Corbishley, M., and M. Cooper. *Real Romans: Digital Time Traveller* (English Heritage/TAG Publishing, 1999).

Cornell, T., and J. Matthews. *Atlas of the Roman World* (Checkmark Books, 1982).

Deckker, Zilah. *Ancient Rome: National Geographic Investigates.* National Geographic Society, 2007.

Green, M. *Roman Archaeology* (Longman, 1983).

Hodge, P. (ed.). *Roman Technology and Crafts* (Aspects of Roman Life Series, Longman, 1979).

James, S. *Ancient Rome* (Dorling Kindersley, 2004).

Macauley, D. *City: A Story of Roman Planning and Construction* (Houghton Mifflin, 1983.

MacDonald, F. *Ancient Rome* (100 Things You Should Know About Series, Barnes & Noble, 2004).

MacKay, C. S. *Ancient Rome: A Military and Political History* (Cambridge University Press, 2007).

Matyszak, P. *Ancient Rome on 5 Denarii a Day* (Thames and Hudson, 2008).

Roberts, P. (ed.). *Ancient Rome* (Discoveries Series, Barnes & Noble, 2003).

Talbert, R. (ed.). *Atlas of Classical History* (Macmillan, 1985).

WEBSITES

http://www.historyforkids.org/
Community service learning project from Portland State University. Click on "Europe" on the map and follow the link to Ancient Rome.

http://www.harcourtschool.com/activity/pompeii/
Harcourt Brace site dedicated to Pompeii.

http://www.silchester.rdg.ac.uk
Up-to-date information about Silchester Roman City.

http://www.romanbaths.co.uk
Web site about the Roman baths at Bath, England.

http://www.hadrians-wall.org
Web site with information and photos about this Roman frontier defense in Britian.

http://www.pbs.org/empires/romans/empire/index.html
PBS Web site about the Roman Empire in the 1st century CE.

http://library.thinkquest.org/22866/English.FRAME.HTML
Web site with many links about ancient Rome.

INDEX